W9-ADC-405

WHEN YOU FIND MY BODY

When You Find My Body

The Disappearance of
Geraldine Largay on the Appalachian Trail

D. Dauphinee

Camden, Maine

Down East Books

An imprint of The Rowman & Littlefield Publishing Group, Inc.
4501 Forbes Blvd, Suite 200
Lanham, MD 20706
www.rowman.com

Distributed by NATIONAL BOOK NETWORK

British Library Cataloguing in Publication Information available
Library of Congress Cataloging-in-Publication Data available

ISBN 978-1-60893-690-8 (hardcover)
ISBN 978-1-60893-691-5 (e-book)

∞™ The paper used in this publication meets the minimum requirements of American National Standard for Information Sciences—Permanence of Paper for Printed Library Materials, ANSI/ NISO Z39.48-1992.

For Raymond Dauphinee Sr.,
who taught me what to do if ever I were lost in a wood

Contents

Author's Note ix

CHAPTER 1 THE GOOD TRAIL 1
CHAPTER 2 TRAIL MAGIC AND ZERO DAYS 17
CHAPTER 3 A HIKE WORTH DOING 23
CHAPTER 4 MAINE 43
CHAPTER 5 OFF THE BEATEN PATH 47
CHAPTER 6 LOST 57
CHAPTER 7 WHAT IS ONE TO DO? 65
CHAPTER 8 THE SEARCH 73
CHAPTER 9 THE WILL TO LIVE 83
CHAPTER 10 ALL LEADS EXPLORED 91
CHAPTER 11 DIG DEEPER, KEEP LOOKING 103
CHAPTER 12 ACQUIESCENCE. 115
CHAPTER 13 LEGACY AND LESSONS 141

Epilogue 171
Acknowledgments 177
About the Author 179

Author's Note

On October 14, 2015, on the eastern slopes of the four-thousand-foot Redington range, just north of the Appalachian Trail in Maine, two contractors were conducting an environmental survey on lands used by the US Navy for its Survival, Evasion, Resistance, and Escape school. Often referred to as the SERE school, the training takes place on a naval property whose southeastern border runs along a section of the Appalachian Trail and is separated only by a corridor of forest about five hundred feet wide.

It was eighty-six degrees that day, hot and humid. The surveyors were young and physically fit and were used to negotiating the steep ravines, the thick, burly cedars, the scrub spruce trees, and dwarf juniper that choke the many small brooks in the area. They were practised at cutting swaths through sections of brush that are so hard going that moose, deer—even rabbits—walk around them. The topographers were cruising through the forest about 10:30 in the morning. At the top of a steep, rounded ridge, they sighted a transect—a fixed path an observer can move along and count certain species of a study, such as plants or animals.

Once the transect line was established between two fixed points, the man operating the transit stepped backward to obtain a bearing, sighting between the two chosen points, like a golfer lining up a shot. On the third or fourth backward step, the young man stepped on something strange—it wasn't a stick. It wasn't a rock. The surveyor looked behind him. It was a collapsed tent. He stood, staring at the ground, analyzing the moment, when he called to his partner: "I think I found that hiker."

They looked around. There, in the scanty shade of a hemlock tree, were the remains of a campsite. There was a small, flattened, black tent with a mustard-yellow rain fly. They inspected the site. Lying near the tent was a green backpack. Near the tent and backpack was a tattered sleeping bag.

The young surveyor peered closer. Inside the bag were some bones. They were unmistakably human.

For the discoverers, it was disconcerting. They collected themselves, snapped a photo of the site for the state police, and created a waypoint of the campsite on their GPS. It was a waypoint of despair. The remains were less than eight hundred yards from the Appalachian Trail.

To the west of the surveyors was the wrong direction home, leading deeper into the forest. To the east, a steep slope led fifty yards downhill to a boulder-strewn brook. They chose a route and made their way out of the dense woods and called their boss at the forest resource and management company they worked for, who called the state police.

DNA testing would later prove what everybody had suspected, and what the head of Maine's official search-and-rescue team, Lieutenant Kevin Adam of the Maine Warden Service, had known to be true: the body on the knoll was that of Geraldine "Gerry" Largay, most recently from Georgia, who had gotten lost two years earlier when she'd left the Appalachian Trail to relieve herself. She had walked off the trail to get out of sight, and, at some point, she'd become disoriented. Had she been distracted by a lovely plant? Did she see an interesting bird? (Gerry loved birds and flora.) Whatever happened, she'd gotten turned around and could not find her way.

Within forty-eight hours of her stepping off the trail, one of the largest, most challenging rescue efforts in the history of the state was under way. Gerry was lost.

In Maine, the warden service has a remarkable 98 percent success rate for finding people lost in the woods. They're good at it, and they pride themselves on it. During the extensive search in 2013 for Appalachian Trail hiker Geraldine Largay, it seemed the entire state of Maine was either emotionally or physically invested in her cause. I, too, was invested.

The book before you is less a biography than a reporting. Perhaps it is an homage. It is meant to celebrate not only Gerry's life but also her spirit of adventure, her yearning for lifelong scholarship, her will to pursue her dream, and her faith. I hope that it will illustrate her journey—and the journeys of those who tried to help her. This book will cover aspects of the Appalachian Trail, the many volunteer searchers, and the Maine Warden Service.

Though I have years of search-and-rescue, medical, wilderness, and expedition experience, I have tried throughout this book to minimize my own opinions and have drawn conclusions based on research from those involved closely with Gerry's ordeal, from testimony of some who knew her well, and from people she met on the trail.

Geraldine Largay was an extremely likeable woman. She seldom complained. Well into her sixties, when some people settle into complacency as they approach seventy, she possessed an insatiable desire for learning. Having never met Gerry, those traits, realized from conversations during my research, have endeared her to me.

Once she became lost in the forest, Gerry's saga was miserable. She was in the thick of it. Nature has the power to save people and to break hearts. There were mistakes made, which will be discussed, but it's important for the reader to understand that for more than three months on the trail, in a difficult environment, and with the considerable help of her devoted husband, George, Gerry more than held her own. Some readers will regard her as simply someone who shouldn't have been hiking alone, and others will debate whether she should have acquired some "woods sense" in addition to her hiking experience. Others might call it a perfect storm of unfortunate events. My deductions, born of two years of research, are rather simple in the end and will be evident in the pages of this book. I invite readers to form their own opinions.

Appalachian Trail hikers have a tradition of adopting "trail names." Please note that to avoid confusion, I have italicized each hiker's trail name throughout this book.

D. Dauphinee, October 2018

CHAPTER ONE

The Good Trail

The forest makes a claim upon men's hearts . . .
that so wonderfully changes and renews a weary spirit.
                                    —ROBERT LOUIS STEVENSON

Tim McElhannon had already hiked hard for five hours in the low, rolling hills of the Mahoosuc Range on the Appalachian Trail in southwestern Maine when he cruised over a hill in the trail and saw a woman sitting on the ground with her pack off. The day was clear and windless, with temperatures in the eighties. The dew point was high, which made it a warm day in the mountains of Maine. The air felt heavy. The songbirds were quiet in the midday heat, and the distant drone of the cicadas made the day seem hotter still. The date was July 17, 2013. Tim stopped to say hi to the woman, and they exchanged greetings. She looked to Tim, who was fifty-six years old, to be a hiker of some age, older than himself. As they shook hands, she introduced herself as "Gerry . . . *Inchworm*," her adopted trail name. Tim noticed that *Inchworm* was a small woman but looked fit for her age. With her short brown hair, black-rimmed glasses, and her ready smile, she graced the trail with a certain style.

"*Walker*," he said, sharing his trail name. "Tim, in the real world." Gerry flashed an effervescent smile.

"I really paused just to say hello," Tim recalls, "to exchange trail names, and to make sure everything was okay with her. I felt she had a special quality about her, so I took off my pack and sat down next to her."

Stopping during a hike was unusual for Tim. A former navy helicopter pilot and instructor at the Virginia Military Institute, he is an athlete, tall and lean. He likes to hike fast, and he likes to keep moving. He is a handsome, high-achieving family man and is kind to strangers—one of those career military men who seem like regular, nice gentlemen but whom you want in your corner if things go south. But Gerry, just by being there, made him slow down and relax. The new acquaintances looked out across the blue and gray hazy landscape at Baldpate Mountain, one more scene of beauty among hundreds along the Appalachian Trail. Both were *thru-hikers*, tackling the entire "AT" in a single season.

"My husband, George, is following along the hike in his car," Gerry told Tim. "I get to spend most nights with him in towns along the way. He'll be waiting for me at the road crossing near Andover. If you want, he can give you a ride into town, and he'll have time to get back and pick me up." She knew her pace. She mentioned that she was hiking slowly and that she had some back pain. Gerry had been hiking on her own for eighteen days.

"Once I was a few miles down the trail," said Tim, "I called the Pine Ellis Lodge in Andover, where *Inchworm* and George would be staying, and made a reservation. The manager offered to meet me at the road crossing, and, not knowing for certain if George would be there, I took him up on it." When Tim reached the crossing, George was there waiting. Tim told him he had met his wife, and they made plans to have dinner together.

Once Gerry and George finally got to the lodge, "Gerry was pretty tired," recalls Tim. He and George picked up some takeout food while Gerry got cleaned up, and they all ate, talked, and watched television at the lodge before calling it an early night. The next morning, Tim rode back to the trailhead with Gerry and George. "Being a faster hiker," reports Tim, "I didn't expect to see them again on the trail." (Tim's daily hiking mileage was about twice that of Gerry's.)

But Tim did see them again, just three days later. *Walker* reached the town of Rangeley on the 19th. "I planned to stop just for the night," remembers Tim, "but there were some severe thunderstorms, so I decided to take a zero day"—those days when no trail miles are logged. "About lunchtime on the 20th, I ran into George at an ice cream shop. We talked for a while, and George said Gerry was scheduled to arrive that evening. He mentioned that Gerry had been hiking with Dianne *Gummy Bear* Cook, a Canadian woman whom I had met on July 4th, outside of Hanover, New Hampshire." Tim had crossed paths with *Gummy Bear* several times on the trail. "I remember being happy that she and Gerry were hiking together," Tim recalls.

At the ice cream shop, Tim and George made plans to have dinner together with Gerry at a popular pizza shop in Rangeley. "We did," said Tim. "We had a great dinner, and we talked a long time." Gerry and George—both gregarious people—opened up to him. They explained to Tim how they'd met and what their plans were for the future. Though they'd raised a family in the Nashville area, George and Gerry had most recently lived in Georgia.

"Gerry wanted to finish her hike and then move to Nashville, where she could be close to her grandchildren," recalled Tim. "She said she wanted to be close to her 'babies.'" Gerry and George were both air force veterans, and Tim was retired from the navy. The three talked for a short time about the military. "We had that connection," says Tim, "but we didn't go into any great detail."

The three made tentative plans for the future. Because Gerry was trekking the northern half of a "flip-flop" hike, she hadn't hiked any part of Virginia yet. Tim lives in that state, in Lexington, about twenty minutes from the AT. "We made plans for them to stay at my house when Gerry would be hiking through my part of Virginia," said Tim. "I told them I would help them with shuttles and give them some local intel" (read: best ice cream places) "and maybe hike a few days with Gerry." George paid for the pizza. "He wouldn't accept any money from me," said Tim. "He was a generous guy. I had such positive feelings about them both. I looked forward to seeing them again some time in the fall, in Virginia."

"The next morning, July 21st," reports Tim, "I had made arrangements for a shuttle to the trailhead. *Postman*, a hiker I had hiked off and on with since North Carolina, arrived at the hotel early to share the shuttle. The shuttle was late, so I called George on his cell phone to see if we could ride with him and Gerry to the trailhead. It went straight to voice mail. I left a message but didn't hear back." The cell service in western Maine is notoriously spotty. It is not unusual to have to travel miles for any reception. "Eventually, the shuttle arrived," said Tim. "Once on the trail, *Postman* and I hiked together for a while, but he had to stop and fix a problem with his pole. I kept on hiking, knowing he'd catch up to me."

About a mile or so later, Tim came upon George and Gerry stopped on the trail. "Hello!" said Tim. "I was happy to see them again and asked them how they were."

"I'm just hiking in with Gerry for a few miles to make sure she's all set—to make sure her water's right, and to make sure she's okay for the next couple of days," said George. (This stretch of trail is rough going, as they say in Maine, and many hikers require two nights to reach the next road crossing, usually staying at the Poplar Ridge and Spaulding Mountain shelters.) They all exchanged hugs, and Tim kept hiking.

"I had a strange feeling after our brief meeting on the trail that something wasn't right with them." Tim recalls, "They weren't as warm and friendly as they had been the night before. I wondered if they were having a disagreement about something." That was the last time he saw Gerry and George on the trail. What couples, married or otherwise, don't have occasional disagreements? It could've been anything: Was George's back hurting? Gerry's? Disagreement on how much water to carry? Had Gerry forgotten something at the hotel? It was just a feeling. Had Tim misread them, and actually all was well? (George would later say that *Inchworm* had told him that the trail was getting harder for her.)

Tim was among the last people to see Gerry alive.

Eighty-seven days earlier, on April 23, 2013, sixty-six-year-old Geraldine Largay and a hiking companion, Jane Lee, had departed north from Harpers Ferry, West Virginia, on their quest to hike the entire Appalachian Trail. It had been an auspicious start. Both women were relatively fit, and though they did not have mountaineering experience, by any means, they had worked hard to acquire the expertise to tackle the physically and mentally tough AT.

Most thru-hikers, like Tim *Walker* McElhannon, are *nobos*—hiking northbound—starting at Springer Mountain in Georgia. About 10–15 percent hike southbound. They are called *sobos*. Both hiking directions have their pros and cons. There are enough overlapping pros, however, that some hikers, like Gerry and Jane, make the decision to attempt a *flip-flop* hike: typically starting at Harpers Ferry, West Virginia, and hiking first to Maine, then traveling back to Harpers Ferry and starting again, hiking the southern half of the trail. The two women were well prepared; Gerry's husband, George, would be driving his Toyota Highlander along the way, helping with equipment, food, and support. Eventually, his adopted trail name would become *Sherpa*. A preexisting back ailment, combined with the fact that an AT thru-hike "wasn't my thing," kept George from attempting the adventure. "This was her hike," he would say. George, like other family members, felt strongly that his wife should not attempt the Appalachian Trail without a companion. Jane Lee, Gerry's hiking friend, would be that companion.

Gerry and Jane had met years earlier when they were members of the Alpharetta Newcomers Group, a multi-interest club in Georgia. They both belonged to the same canasta club.

"When I was hosting the group at my house," said Jane, "I overheard Gerry talking about going on a hiking trip in the Smokies. I asked if I could join her, and the rest is history."

Gerry Largay, born Geraldine Burnite, grew up in a family of modest means in Tampa, Florida. Graced with an infectious smile and love of learning, she easily made friends. One of her earliest and closest childhood friends was Betty Anne Ferguson. Gerry and Betty Anne were in the Girl Scouts together and went to the same high school. Still active in the Girl Scouts while in high school, Gerry would play the ukulele on campouts for sing-alongs with the Scouts. "Our singing probably wasn't great, but it was so much fun when she played the ukulele," says Betty Anne. "I'm not sure if she actually knew any chords, but it sounded good."

After high school, Betty Anne was off to Hollins College in Virginia, eventually becoming an ornithologist. Gerry went to nursing school at Grady Hospital in Atlanta. "We kept close with letters throughout college and spent precious time together when home during holidays," said Betty Anne. It was a friendship that never waned. Later in life, they went on many vacations together, often with their spouses. Several times Gerry accompanied Betty Anne on her field studies abroad, researching tropical birds. According to Betty Anne—whose married name by then was Schreiber (later Schenk)—"Gerry had great enthusiasm for learning anything new and was always enjoyable to be around." On one trip to the South Pacific, studying red-tailed tropicbirds, Gerry had to carry banding materials, pens, notebooks, and a towel, so she found some fabric and sewed huge, clownish, oversized pockets onto her khaki shorts. "Those shorts looked so silly, but Gerry didn't care," Betty Anne remembers.

In her last year of nursing school, Gerry enlisted in the air force. After graduation, when stationed in California, she met George Largay, who worked in hospital administration. By all accounts, George took one look at Gerry and fell hard. They were eventually married, and as George pursued a career in marketing, Gerry would find nursing jobs in each town. And those who knew them well agree: they were a lovely couple.

Gerry and George traveled extensively, often with Betty Anne and her husband. (Unfortunately, Betty Anne became a widow quite early in life, and she later remarried.) The couples visited the Galápagos, Normandy, Machu Picchu, Burgundy, and other destinations. According to Betty Anne, "Gerry loved learning about the places and was a skilled navigator through Europe. Even during the odd times when traveling can be stressful, Gerry remained positive. She was always upbeat, and she was funny."

We can best be measured by the close friends we have in life, and these are the attributes Gerry's friends speak of, time and again. It is apparent when speaking to those who knew her best that Gerry loved purely and completely.

"Gerry would volunteer to help with tropical-bird research when we banded and weighed the seabirds in colonies of thousands. She didn't mind being bitten and shit on," remembers Betty Anne. Gerry was not prideful and not overburdened with self-awareness. "She truly loved nature—just being out in it—but she really liked the birds," says Betty Anne. "When she hiked, she often took along some guidebooks, for birds and for flora . . . though she probably didn't want the weight on the Appalachian Trail."

Betty Anne still struggles to talk about her friend. Some of the friends in Gerry's inner circle still can't talk about her. "It seemed as though she cared about everyone and everything," Betty Anne says, chuckling and pausing for a long moment. "Even quilting. Her quilts were elaborate, and every stitch meant something."

As Gerry thoroughly researched hiking the Appalachian Trail, she undoubtedly became aware of the hardships she would endure. She knew about the slogging, wet days to come, the hunger, the threat of dehydration. She understood. She prepared herself, and the challenges only enriched her dream to attempt the hike. She dared to dream, and she dared to try. During the two years preparing for her AT attempt, Gerry kept a journal, which she shared with friends through e-mails and letters. While training for her hike, long before she would have the trail name *Inchworm*, she sent out an update. Betty Anne's e-mail read,

OK, everyone!

Wednesday, November 7th we head to Amicalola Lodge to spend the night—and begin our practice trek to Burningtown Gap, NC, 124.4 miles north, the next morning. This is 36 miles short of what we hoped to do—but it has taken forever to get the house ready—and then to figure out how to pack ourselves in the most economical way. One of the first problems encountered is that our new iPads don't do distribution lists. Geez—all that technology and then what good is it?? So our email updates will go to daughter, Kerry, who will forward to all of you. The subject line will read "Team Gerry" which is how I regard you all—thanks to Ken and Joyce who put the term in henna tattoos

*on their arms in September when we saw them in the mountains!
Those tats last 3 weeks, did you know?!*

*This has been a long time in the planning and we are excited and
a little nervous to begin this adventure. This one is all about finding
each other at the end of each day. The one in June with Jane and Kit
was to test out our equipment and experience what two weeks on the
AT was actually like. For those who may not know, a 26 pound pack in
June was nearly intolerable to me due to multiple back issues. Warren
worked with us for the better part of two days helping us learn how
George could meet me at a road crossing nearly every night and thereby
carry a big portion of my load in the car. Jen and Brew worked with
us especially on the matter of what it means to be a support person. So
George's trail name is Sherpa—mine is yet to be determined.*

*We will send a few updates during these 11 days—please feel free
to let me know if you would just as soon not have our emails cram
your inbox. I am fairly certain that I am only including those who
have asked. If I included you in error, please let me know. Also, we'd
love to hear from those so inclined—you can use either my email or
George's—glargay2010@gmail.com.*

*Best!
Gerry, the AT Dreamer*

Four months later, Betty Anne received another update:

AT update from Inchworm and Sherpa

*Trail names officially chosen! I have picked Inchworm as that is
exactly how I feel going up any ascent. No matter how well I feel I'm
doing, I am always humbled anew on the ups. Sherpa is perfect for
George except he has a car, not a llama.*

*For those of you who read about our Georgia trek, go on to the
next paragraph. For those new to our list, here is a very brief sum-
mary: hiked from Springer Mtn, the southern terminus of the AT, to
Deep Gap, NC, 85.5 miles in 7 days. Beautiful fall weather, chilly*

nights, short days. Glorious views as no leaves on the trees. George has the heavier stuff in the car so my backpack is lighter. He hikes in with me each morning for at least an hour, doubles back to the car, drives to our afternoon road crossing where he can leave the car, and hikes in to finish the hike with me. A pretty good plan except the forest service roads can be tricky, to say the least.

Third, and final, practice hike began on February 27. (First hike was in June with 2 girlfriends ... about 150 miles from Damascus, VA to Hot Springs, NC. Did not cover every mile of that section so will repeat when the real adventure begins. It was great though as we learned what days on the trail really meant ... and how we liked our equipment. Some real aha-s). We drove to Hiawassee, GA on Feb 26 with the intention of hiking NC from where we left off in Nov at Deep Gap to Fontana Dam.

First morning, tried to drive to starting point only to find forest road to trailhead gated and double locked. Big disappointment. Couldn't go to the end point and start as Geo couldn't have picked me up at other end. New plan. Went north a bit to a new starting point. Planned to hike 10.1. George met me much earlier on trail than expected as he had not been able to get in on the forest road to pick me up at agreed-upon finish. Ran into an energy truck driver actually unlocking that gate who told him that many forest roads are closed off in winter due to snow, ice, mud. (The energy guy was going in to service some facility problem). Who would have guessed. Paltry 5.1 miles. Called it a day, made new plan. The next day drove way farther north to Wesser, NC, Nantahala Outdoor Center. We decided on this as the next 2 starts were on major roads.

This segment of trail northward to Stecoah Gap is 13.4 miles. It ascends 3300 feet in 8 miles up to 5062. So plenty of time to easily go up before you go down, right? Except we began at 30 degrees and the temp drops 3 degrees for every 1000 feet. George turned back after 1.5 hrs to go drive to the ending point. As I ascended, the snow grew thicker and the wind was more piercing depending on the turn of the mountain. It was the first time I have been a bit scared ... what if the snow thickened so that I would not be able to see? The hoarfrost was amazing . . . the most fantastic so far, as far as I could see. (Hoarfrost: a deposit of needle-like ice crystals formed by direct condensation @ temps below freezing). The caps froze on my water bottles and my power bar was solid. I was able to get the bottles open easily and found ice crystals in my water. Geez, I was COLD. And I couldn't sit to rest because that made me colder. I made it to Cheoah Bald in 5 hours (way slow), then at least I could begin to descend. George ended up doing a few extra miles to meet up with me. We finished at 6:15 . . . almost 10 hours. The car never looked so good.

The next day was to be another 13.4 . . . but we decided that we might hold the AT for a day. So we went into the Smokies and did 12 miles on a fairly easy stretch. Felt great. Then the weather really turned sour, and today we are relaxing at Fontana Dam lodge. Glad to be here. Will take on that 13.4 miles tomorrow!

So that's a lot of words, but it's been an experience. And did I say that we had a flat tire on the drive up to Hiawassee!? Yikes. More in a few days . . .

Months later, when she stood at a crossroads in New Hampshire, *Inchworm* and George would have a decision to make: Gerry—who had a fear of the dark and of being alone—would dare to continue on her hike by herself. She was brave.

A few weeks before starting her Appalachian adventure, Gerry and George drove to Asheville and stayed a few nights with Betty Anne and her husband. "BA" (as Gerry sometimes referred to her in correspondence) confirmed with Gerry via e-mail:

Dear G,

I have you down for the nights of 18, 19, 20. Is that correct?
It's a perfect time to come! the garden should look great, dogwoods out maybe? And we can hike the Largay Loop!! Chris and Iain are

coming from England in Oct. and want to work on a trail—so they can have a named trail like you!! So you can see where we want to lay out a new one.

Will be great to have you here for a bit!!

I'm off to a planning meeting . . . then we are meeting friends we sponsor our wine tasting with to taste some wines and have dinner.

XOX
BA

Gerry responded:

Sounds like great fun! Was afraid we might intrude. Would love to do it all. Started to think if there were any way we'd be near Asheville when Chris & Iain are there, would be such fun to see them. We'll just see how this whole gig goes! . . .

Will be so good to see you. Way too long.

XOX Gerry

Through their correspondence, it's obvious that Betty Anne and Gerry had a very special relationship, and one can sense their lifelong affection. If we're lucky, like them, we make many friends in our lifetime, but those friendships that endure from childhood seem different. They get more comfortable and are treasured more with each passing year.

For Gerry, "the AT Dreamer," those first few steps along the trail from Harpers Ferry were a dream come true. It was a familiar dream that is shared by thousands of people every year, decade after decade, but realized by few. For each hiker, it is an intensely personal, and very old, shared dream that began eighty-eight years before Gerry first set foot on the trail, on March 3, 1925, when twenty-six outdoor enthusiasts met at the beautiful white granite and marble Raleigh Hotel in Washington, D.C. It was unseasonably hot for early spring. The minutes of the meeting show the gathering was informal. However, out of that meeting grew an association and from that a movement that would become an enduring force—a rare, successful marriage of human being and nature. The meeting was organized by a rather straight-laced, otherwise unassuming "Harvard man" who came across as an upper-level bureaucrat. Benton MacKaye, a forester and a regional planner who would be consumed by the zeitgeist in the years following World War I, when the world was trying to figure out the order of things and organizations, associations, and clubs were all the rage. MacKaye wanted to form an all-volunteer organization charged with building the Appalachian Trail. He was then, and still is, regarded somewhat as a dreamer.

MacKaye's dream of the Appalachian Trail may have been born of a lack of connection to any community in his youth. His childhood seems to have been absent a sense of place. His father was an actor, or "dramatist," who dabbled in a half-dozen business ventures, all of which failed. The family was forced to move around to different towns and was at least twice destitute. The MacKayes stayed at a few farms while trying to get established. Reading between the lines of early family writings, there are hints that the clan may have stayed a brief time in at least one city farm. Common in the late 1800s, *city farms*—sometimes called "almshouses"—were established to give the poor of local communities a place to work for room and board until they could get their affairs in order. The slang term was "the poorhouse." Eventually, when Benton was nine years old, the family settled at a farmstead his older brother William had purchased in Shirley Center, Massachusetts, about thirty minutes' drive from Boston. Likely already affected by moving around so often, Benton found solace and happiness in nature, spending much of his free time walking and hiking in the forests near Shirley. He and some childhood friends even created what they called the Rambling Boys' Club. The club's credo might shine a light on MacKaye's future endeavors: "To give the members an education of the lay of the land in which they live, also of other lands, taking in the geography, geology, zoology, and botany of them." The young future regional planner had found his sense of place in nature. When his brother William died unexpectedly—possibly from a respiratory infection—the family finally moved to Washington, D.C.

MacKaye's concepts were somewhat different from what the AT would eventually become. He first wrote about the idea in 1921 for an article in the *Journal of the American Institute of Architects*, titled "An Appalachian Trail: A Project in Regional Planning." This article outlined the author's plan for sections of trails meeting up from state to state along the Appalachian crest. He also expounded on his grave concerns about the alarming shift—at least to him—of the rural population to urban areas, the lack of available employment in the United States, a new sense of American development and purpose, and of rural community building. In the article, perhaps for perspective, he described his vision of the lands from the view of a giant. Being so tall, MacKaye's giant could see potential in the landscape where others might not. He was daring the readers—and the metaphoric Brobdingnagian—to dream with him.

Word spread among the outdoor enthusiasts of the East, especially between New York and Washington. MacKaye began spreading the word about his Appalachian Trail quest.

As interest in the idea grew, one of the outdoor enthusiasts who became involved was Arthur Perkins, a judge from Hartford, Connecticut. While an attorney, Perkins had become an ardent hiker, climbing and hiking throughout New England, especially in New Hampshire. In 1925, he had carved out enough time from his law career to become involved in trail work and, in 1928, was named acting chairman of the Appalachian Trail Conservancy. Perkins had a devoted protégé, a maritime lawyer named Myron Avery, who had grown up on the coast of Maine. Beyond being an outdoor enthusiast and a serious "walker," Avery was a bona fide explorer, making tracks into many parts of the East Coast that at the time were still regarded as wilderness. The young attorney looked—and acted—every bit the nineteenth-century adventurer. Had he been born twenty, fifty, or seventy-five years earlier, he might have been exploring the Northwest Passage or racing Roald Amundsen and Robert F. Scott to the South Pole. Men like Myron Avery and explorers before him are typically born leaders, but they are men who often leave in their wake bruised egos, and Avery would inflict his share. Whether they ruffle feathers or not, the best explorers lead by example, and Avery did just that. It is likely that Judge Perkins influenced Avery to become involved with the AT. Regardless of how Avery's interest in the project started, it would change everything in the building of the trail.

As much as everyone agrees that Benton MacKaye dreamed up the trail, it should be agreed that Myron Avery built it. MacKaye's ideas about linking existing trail systems together to create a communal, utopic social entity would evolve significantly between 1920 and 1930. While MacKaye was often perceived as a "dignified, affable philosopher with the ever-present pipe clamped between his teeth," Avery was a hard-nosed, get-it-done attorney. Avery grew up in Lubec, Maine, in Washington County, within a family who made their money from sardine packing, in a part of Maine where the citizens were too busy surviving to do much philosophizing. Avery was a child in a place that was often left out of conversations in the state's political circles, and where there was little development, growth, and jobs. People from "Downeast" Maine must be resilient, and they must be tough. Avery, though congenial enough, certainly grew up tough.

If not for Myron Avery, the AT might have officially ended in New Hampshire, on the summit of Mount Washington, as the early plans intended. But by 1924, a proposal was made for the trail to extend to the summit of Mount Katahdin. Much of Maine—especially the mountainous region along the western part of the state—was true wilderness. It was Avery who believed the wilderness experience would enrich the Appalachian Trail.

Along the Maine–New Hampshire border were farms and hamlets, but the farther north one traveled, the more remote it was; even game wardens rarely ventured there. Hiking only eighty miles north on the proposed trail toward Katahdin, you were on your own.

The AT has no soul, but it may seem at times like it does—as if it were a living, breathing thing. Søren Kierkegaard wrote, "The thing is that which in itself is becoming." By its ever-changing manner, the trail continues to evolve in the minds of hikers and admirers. The complexion of the trail changes with the weather and with the man-made structures along its course, both good and bad; it zigs and zags this way and that annually. The maps of the trail often change slightly, but the direction remains the same.

People from all walks of life attempt the AT every year, with more than two thousand attempting a thru-hike. One in four thru-hikers reports a completed hike. As many as three million people annually hike a section of the Appalachian National Scenic Trail. Eighty-seven percent of thru-hikers choose the traditional northbound—nobo—route. Almost anyone can at least attempt it. To quote Sir Edmund Hillary, "Adventuring can be for the ordinary person with ordinary qualities, such as I regard myself." Ed might have been ordinary, but he was a man of focus. Some seek a challenge; some want the natural beauty; some simply want to breathe fresh air. The trail *can* lead to renewal, understanding, growth, discovery—even redemption, which can be a fickle thing.

Gerry Largay was in no need of redemption or growth. She was simple in her intentions; she embraced the challenge of seeing the thing through.

Chapter Two

Trail Magic and Zero Days

Civilized life has kept me busy.
—Terry Bliss (*Blue Moon*), 2013 (blog entry)

It's not worthwhile asking AT thru-hikers why they're doing it. The answers never seem to offer any real clarity. You can seldom hear the tone of another person's soul, except through music or poetry, and typically the reasons a hiker attempts a thru-hike are intensely personal. I try not to ask thru-hikers the puerile question. Gerry Largay hiked the trail for the challenge and for the adventure of it all. Though she was in her mid-sixties, she had a "youthful enthusiasm for learning and experiencing things," as one friend remembers. There is beauty in advanced age, just as there is in youth. Triumph over the challenges we face and absorbing the profound beauty in nature are some of the most wonderful experiences humans can have; Appalachian Trail hikers get both. Effervescence flows from those who enjoy life, those who smile as often as Gerry did and live with passion. Those are the people who light up the lives of others.

All trails are unexplored to those hiking them for the first time, so the prospects are boundless. A hiker's very presence on the Appalachian Trail is an act of affection, even when the trail beats you down.

Often Appalachian Trail hikers are people in transition. They might be graduating from college, retiring, or divorcing. Even folks who have recently been released from prison attempt it. There are those showing the world they've beaten a disease or just celebrating inwardly. Some simply want to lose weight or get into shape. Whatever the reason, hiking the Appalachian Trail is enriching—if you allow it to be.

The AT is populated nearly every year with the elderly, preteens, the diabetic, the amputated, the cancer-stricken, the healthy, the deaf . . . the blind. Along the way, the hikers are inevitably moved by the culture of the trail. For me, in my twenties, I was drawn to trails because of the forests. Some people feel that the forest has immeasurable value for all humans. In the woods, the sharp corners of life's considerations and conflicts are simplified by the minimalism of one's surroundings. Deeper in the forest is an opening for our hostilities to drift away. The wilderness offers an escape into a refuge from civilization, while at once being harsh and hostile. It forces us to recognize our frailty. As a section hiker (to date, 1,241 miles), my exposure to trail culture has been different from that of thru-hikers, but I witnessed kindness along the way. I noticed the diversity of people; I heard the music and listened to the stories. I even experienced the "rebel yell" one morning while a sheltermate from the night before relieved himself behind the lean-to. (We had previously talked into the night about the Civil War.) It's quite possible that it wasn't really a rebel yell; he may have been experiencing a bad case of dysuria. In those early days, I happily experienced the camaraderie and thought it was cool, but as I took longer, extended trips, I came to understand the beauty of the trail culture.

Years after my first experiences on the Appalachian Trail, Gerry Largay would have her own varied experiences on many of the same sections of trail. The people she met, the advice she received, the friendships she made, and the conversations she had influenced and buoyed her. She would despair over the incessant rainfall in the June of her AT hike but would be lifted by the beauty of the wet ferns and the comforting words of a new acquaintance. She would run into hikers with similar life experiences and vent about the evolution of medicine in America. Even in retirement, she still advocated for the well-being of patients.

The people I met on the AT from the cities loved nature because it offered the potential for transcendent growth, and on the Appalachian Trail they could breathe the air and see the stars at night. Many go to slip the restrictions of the homogeneous suburban or urban environment they live in. The farm boys on the trail felt more at home in the woods but were able to experience the exotic and beautiful unshaved, make-upless women who were not judgmental of the young men when they interacted with them. The farm boys were invigorated. There was growth on the trail.

What's known as "trail magic" is interesting in itself: it is the acts of kindness thru-hikers may encounter along the AT. It can come in many forms: free room and board, coolers with soft drinks on ice left beside the trail, an offer of a ride into town, a shower—a meal. Trail magic is sometimes random and sometimes planned out meticulously. People who offer trail magic are referred to as *trail angels*. There are trail angels who plan their weekends and vacations around providing treats or comfort to thru-hikers.

In the early days, trail magic also referred to the beautiful, regenerative feeling one often gets when confronted with a particularly lovely sight or experience. As far back as the 1970s, when trail magic was becoming prevalent, trail angels were often former thru-hikers, people who understood the tribulations of the AT. Perhaps they had experienced some kindness on their hike and wanted to give back in some way. And that's still very much the case, but, over time, all types of hikers, outdoors people, and those who live in towns or on farms along the trail have become trail angels, and their contributions vary in hundreds of ways. The Appalachian Trail seems to suck the animosity out of people.

Along the AT, contrary to urban lifestyles, competition for camping spots, resources, and "things" are replaced with trust and mutuality. People even take on new identities on the trail, assuming trail names given to them by other hikers or friends. Accepting trail names from friends comes with its own set of concerns; hikers have been saddled with names like *Itchy, Dingleberry, Vulture Chow, Weasel, Rat Puke, Monkeybutt,* and *Snotrocket.* The worst part is that *Dingleberry* and *Snotrocket* were a couple—I don't see any way for the woman to come out rosy there (assuming there was a woman). Some handles are hard to live down. There are hikers who—perhaps wisely—give themselves their own moniker. But that's okay . . . on the AT there is supposed to be no judging. Early on in their adventure, emboldened by their new identities, thru-hikers often assume a new persona to go along with them, sometimes complete with different outlooks and philosophies— even morals.

In addition to assuming trail names along the AT, another way for hikers to identify themselves involves their chosen method of following blazes on the trail. Blazes are painted marks on the trees and stones that designate the path of the trail. The most famous are the white blazes, which indicate the official path of the Appalachian Trail. Those hikers who pass all the white blazes are considered purists. A "blue blazer" is a hiker who hikes only—or some of—the blue blazes, which indicate alternate routes along the AT. While there is supposed to be an unwritten, nonjudgmental rule on the trail—"Hike your own hike"—some of the purists can get a bit elitist, viewing blue blazers and section hikers as having less honor. Blue blazers, however, feel their hike is less restrained than a purist's, and the blue-blaze hike allows more freedom and enjoyment. These distinctions are among the few cases of umbrage on the AT.

Then there are "yellow blazers," hikers who employ the art of hitch-hiking. Some are compelled to hitchhike because of an injury; some are perfectly healthy and are simply cheating (as far as a completed thru-hike is concerned). However, it's important to distinguish between a yellow blazer and those hikers—purists or not—who hitch a ride into nearby trail towns to resupply or for "zero days." Almost every hiker does that.

If that's not enough, there are also "slack packers." They are hikers who may, for whatever reason, use transportation routinely to help them along the way. If they plan well, slack packers can day hike much of the AT. Slack packers are considered by many purists to be just that—slackers. I don't judge anyone for how they want to hike the Appalachian Trail. I don't believe Benton MacKaye would approve of judging. It should be all about the beauty and the hiker's own journey.

There is an overwhelming charm, even a glory, to the Appalachian Trail, and many of the typical social boundaries and limits found in mainstream society are absent. Hikers seem to be able to dress as they want (if they dress at all). I have seen men in kilts, which is always okay, but I've also seen men in skirts. I suppose skirts are lightweight and dry easily, but a fellow has to have the legs to pull it off.

By 1940, more Americans were hiking, and the trail became a reality as MacKaye, Avery, Perkins, and others had envisioned it. In 1948, the first thru-hiker, World War II veteran Earl Shaffer, may have been the first to institute an ethos on the trail of clearing one's head, or as a remedy for the drudgery of normal life. Shaffer was a forward radioman in the 342nd Bomber Squadron in the South Pacific in 1945. He lost two of his closest friends in the war, one of them in the landings at Iwo Jima. The veteran wrote that he wanted to "walk the war out of my system." In his book *Walking with Spring*, Shaffer makes it clear: the Appalachian Trail helped.

The culture of the AT became a movement that was fueled further by Edward Garvey in the early 1970s. Garvey, an engineer recently retired from the Soil Conservation Service, was very active in the Potomac Appalachian Trail Club (like Myron Avery before him) and with the Appalachian Trail Conservancy. He made his thru-hike in 1970. That year, there were only nine other thru-hikers. The same year, he wrote a book about his journey, *Appalachian Hiker: Adventure of a Lifetime*. Included in the book was his first interaction with nudists—a group he encountered along the trail. He explains in his book, "I could not get a good look at the second person. However, when I drew abreast—and I choose that word carefully—I saw that the second person was a very curvaceous young lady, and she was not wearing dungarees, nor was she wearing anything else! She seemed a little new to the nudist game and somewhat ill at ease. As I came within speaking distance, she giggled and said, 'Nice day, huh?' I smiled and replied with an enthusiastic, 'Indeed it is!'"

Soon after Garvey's book was published, the number of thru-hikers soared. I wonder if that woman realizes her contribution to the popularity of the Appalachian Trail. Regardless, the book was widely read, and it helped drive the cultural evolution of the AT.

CHAPTER THREE

A Hike Worth Doing

How many things would you attempt if you knew you could not fail?
—ROBERT FROST

Gerry and George Largay and Jane Lee had a plan that was simple enough. They chose the classic flip-flop thru-hike. George would drive the route, skipping ahead of the two friends, and chauffeur them to their accommodations. "This is her hike," he'd repeat, but his involvement was a helpful way of participating. Indeed, his involvement could very well be the recipe for success for the two women; Gerry, though fit and quickly gaining hiking experience, was no youngster. Some mornings, George would take short hikes in for a mile or so with his wife and Jane, or he'd hike in a similar distance from the other end to meet them as they finished for the day. Otherwise, he acted as their one-man support crew.

Gerry's quest for adventures and physical goal setting came later in life, once her family had been raised. Three years before her Appalachian Trail hike, she trained for and ran the Country Music Half Marathon in Nashville, finishing in a time of 2:57:56. Not fast, but most sixty-three-year-old Americans will never try it. But Gerry's interest in the outdoors started early. Betty Anne Schenk does not remember a time when Gerry wasn't enthralled with the out-of-doors and everything that lives in it.

After running the half marathon in 2010, Gerry's late-life goal setting continued. Like so many others do each year, she set her sights on the Appalachian Trail. She planned. She trained. She read books. She talked to hikers. She weighed her equipment in measurements of grams. She and hiking buddy Lee went to several "hiking camps" in the years before their attempt of the AT. In September 2011, Gerry and George took a hiking course taught by Warren Doyle at the Appalachian Trail Institute in eastern Tennessee. The "Institute" is an interesting place, mostly because Doyle is an interesting dude.

Having grown up in a blue-collar family in Connecticut, Doyle attended the University of Connecticut as a theater major. While an undergrad, he volunteered in a West Virginia community-development project and became greatly influenced by Appalachian poet, activist, and possible communist Don West. West was a brave man who questioned authority and wrote some lyrical, concise poetry in which he continually returned to certain favorite themes. West wrote about the "Circle" of the southern states and the power of the circle of fellowship.

Later, while in grad school at UConn in 1973, Doyle felt compelled to "find out who I really was." He decided to try by hiking the Appalachian Trail. That notion is common enough, but Doyle decided to attach his name to the AT; he wanted to set the first speed record. He did the hike conventionally enough—backpack, hiking during daytime hours, campfires at night—and reached the summit of Mount Katahdin in just over sixty-six days—indeed, a new record. He made news (perhaps his real goal) and stirred detractors, especially from the traditional hiking community. Regardless of the odd ridicule he received from some hikers (including a harsh reproach from Himself, Benton MacKaye) for making a "contest" out of the venerable trail, Doyle did seem to get a lot out of the experience. Two years later, he recruited more than a dozen UConn students to hike the AT as a group. They all made it to the summit of Katahdin, which is remarkable, considering that then, as now, only one in four thru-hikers completes the journey. It was Doyle's experimental "Circle Expedition" in which the group—the entire group—was the thing. The whole group would succeed, or the expedition would fail.

That first UConn group served as the basis for Doyle's doctoral thesis, and he tried another Circle Expedition three years later, in 1977, and yet another in 1980. He took some time off from running AT trips to raise a family but started up again in 1990, running Circle Expeditions every five years. The two expectations listed on the Appalachian Trail Institute website for the Appalachian Trail (Circle) Expeditions are as follows:

1. Everyone will walk the entire Appalachian Trail from Georgia to Maine.

2. Everyone will start and finish the trail at the same time.

Pretty simple. But there are really more expectations. For instance, every white blaze must be followed. Another expectation is that group members follow Doyle's orders.

There are those who say that only a few, if any, of the Doyle expedition members will "hike their own hike" (remember the AT mantra). Instead, they hike Doyle's hike. I get that, but it's not entirely true: The folks in his class know what they're doing. They signed up for *his* hike, so they're owning it. He uses a support vehicle, shuttling the hikers' gear along the trail, much to the chagrin of traditional thru-hikers. He's extremely outspoken and opinionated, and he loves to bend rules.

Warren Doyle also founded the Appalachian Long Distance Hikers Association (ALDHA) and is a lifelong member. The scuttlebutt is that Doyle has fallen out of favor with the ALDHA in recent years, and much of it stemmed from when, immediately after 9/11, at a conference at Dartmouth College, Doyle read a poem (the rumor is that it was a Don West poem) and basically said that "America had it coming." In the audience, there was a lot of gnashing of teeth. One of the beautiful things about the Appalachian Trail is the diversity of the masses it attracts, and the ALDHA is made up of AT hikers from many walks of life. For many of the members present, it was not the time or place to make such a political statement.

Much of what Doyle says and does raises the ire of the Appalachian Trail Conservancy (ATC).

Brian King, executive at the ATC and a longtime acquaintance of Warren Doyle, said in 2017, "There are some good things about Warren's point of view, and you've got to hand it to him—he's hiked the AT an awful lot of times."

After a pause, I thought I saw the slightest hint of a stilted smile as King summed up Doyle in six words: "Warren likes to stir things up."

On his guided AT hikes (paid guiding is not allowed on the AT), Doyle adheres to a very strict schedule, which is contrary to many thru-hikers' Thoreau-riddled mind-sets; for them, a head-down, focused-on-the-mileage attitude seems like a waste of perfectly good hiking.

In my younger years, when I was leading expeditions to mountains and jungles in the Far East, Central and South America, Africa, or the Arctic, I looked for people (members) who would be good in a tight spot and cheerful in all weathers—especially if things went to hell. I wanted people who could take over if I were killed but could also accept delegated duties. Men and women who could take the pain and smile. Would I have taken Warren Doyle on one of my trips? Before I met him, I couldn't be sure; everybody had an opinion about him. I might've even rolled my eyes. But, independent of his antics and the way he hikes with his groups, I believe he's correct in much of what he says regarding what it takes to be successful on the AT if you're into peak bagging. He has, after all, hiked the trail almost every way conceivable—and hiked it at least seventeen times. Doyle was very good to me, answering all my questions, and he helped me a great deal. If you are inclined to reserve judgment on people, he's a funky, interesting guy. And he's a hoofer at heart. He also teaches a dance class.

Through decades of promotion and hard-core hiking, Doyle has carved out a niche for himself in Appalachian Trail lore and legend. If one puts aside any of the outspoken abrasiveness he sometimes displays (which is completely subjective), perhaps the most telling fact one should consider is this record: 75 percent of those hikers who attend his Appalachian Trail Institute in eastern Tennessee—the same course Gerry Largay and George attended—succeed in thru-hiking the AT. That is truly astounding.

When speaking about it, Warren Doyle seems to love the Appalachian Trail with all his heart and perhaps as much as any person alive. But people profess their love in many ways.

The Appalachian Trail Institute course was four days long. Katharine Armijo, a photographer from Louisiana, attended the same course as

Gerry and George. She remembers it fondly. "At the ATI, we had days that were split between classroom-type discussion as well as day hikes on the AT," she recalls. "Warren's classroom consisted of several folding tables set up in a large semicircle. I remember Gerry would sit for most of the class wearing her painter's hat and jacket (Warren was no fan of heat or AC) with her hands interlocked and resting on the table. George was always by her side, listening attentively and taking notes. I was so impressed in his support of her. George made it very clear that he would not be hiking but that he was there to help out Gerry and be her support person."

Katharine recalls, "At the course, on the days we hiked, Gerry practically bounced down the trail. She had some energy! That is one thing that has really stuck out in my mind, how she almost caught air with her stride and the big smile on her face with literally every step. It was obvious to me that she was in her element. Gerry didn't seem to know a ton about hiking or equipment at that point (she was there to learn) but sure seemed to have the passion."

The December before her AT hike, Gerry purchased the entire set of official AT maps from the Appalachian Trail Conservancy.

Brian King, the publisher at the Conservancy who oversees books and maps and the sales operation, believes they're important.

"We're not just trying to sell maps," said King in 2017. "We recommend everyone hiking the AT get the maps of each section. If you must get off the trail—or are lost—you think, *I'll follow the drainage downhill, like I'm supposed to* . . . and look at the maps only to find out that it might not be a good idea. There might be a swamp, or maybe it's someone's back yard who's not going to be friendly."

"Some wilderness proponents have been unhappy with our maps," said King, "because we show all towns, roads—even subdivisions. But that's why we show it; okay, you can go here and get help, or you don't want to go here seeking help. Also, with a map, you can tell people where you are if you *do* get cell service."

"Unfortunately," said King, "as many thru-hikers move along the trail, meeting different people, hikers often adjust their hiking plans. Hikers will say, 'Oh, you don't need them . . . just follow the well-marked trail.' Once they get comfortable with that approach, the maps sometimes get left behind. Part of the culture, part of the mind-set, becomes, 'No, I don't need the maps. I haven't needed them yet.'"

Armed with knowledge from her books and the blogs they read, reinforced by Doyle's course, and with a carefully stripped-down gear list, *Inchworm* was close to ready. Gerry and George spent some added time with Doyle, who helped them rough out an itinerary for the thru-hike. Gerry, standing five feet, five inches tall, and weighing only 115 pounds, and occasionally suffering from a nagging back problem herself, knew she wouldn't be comfortable carrying the thirty- to thirty-five-pound pack typical for most thru-hikers. Doyle highlighted maps with every place where roads crossed the trail. The controversial "AT Guru" (some people call Doyle "Yoda of the AT" . . . metaphors be with you) went above and beyond, helping the couple work out a plan that would work for them both. George would be Gerry's and Jane's main support. He would meet them at every feasible point. George was so important to the plan, it was almost as though he were hiking the trail with them.

When starting a flip-flop hike on the AT, it's easy to get distracted by Harpers Ferry, provided you're interested in history. The town reeks of it. Thomas Jefferson stayed there several times on his way to stir up trouble in Philadelphia. George Washington spent time there in 1785, surveying the area for consideration of constructing bypass canals. Nine years later, Washington proposed the US government build one of its two armory and arsenals at Harpers Ferry. They were indeed built, and sixty years later abolitionist John Brown seized the armory at Harpers Ferry. In 1859, with his ragtag group of men, he planned on taking the armory and arming slaves all along the Appalachians with the stolen weapons. They would strike south, calling for all slaves to rise up, and together they would abolish slavery in the country once and for all. It was an ambitious plan. Among his captives was Colonel Lewis Washington—George's great-grandnephew. However, Brown and his band didn't get far. The slaves in Harpers Ferry were petrified of Brown, who was wild-eyed and and seemed a little bit crazy. Brown was captured and hanged in the end. Four years later, slavery was indeed outlawed, and abolition went into effect at the end of the War Between the States.

The town of Harpers Ferry changed hands between the Union and the Confederacy several times during the Civil War, but within a year after the end of the conflict, the reunited United States did something remarkable on the top of the hill overlooking downtown: it opened a college for black students. Storer College originally operated as a normal school to train black educators. It was paid for by philanthropic Baptists from New England—many from Maine. The school stayed open until 1955, when the US Supreme Court ruled in *Brown v. Board of Education* that segregated public schools were unconstitutional. The college stayed vacant for a year until the National Park Service acquired it. The beautiful old buildings now house various training and administrative buildings for the Park Service. The Appalachian Trail Conservancy headquarters are adjacent to the school, but the building feels like part of its fabric. To this day, the old school still has an air of college campus about it.

Gerry Largay no doubt was interested in the town, as most people are, but she was focused on the hike. Her impeccable planning and preparation had steeled her for this adventure, and it was a decent start. On April 23, she and Jane stopped at the ATC headquarters, located on Washington Street, near the top of the hill where the road plunges down into the congested town center. Most hikers stop as a kind of pilgrimage and take a picture of themselves outside the front window. The photos are logged as a rudimentary record of who's hiking the AT, and when. The two women opted not to get their photo taken. Since they were flip-flop hiking, they would have their photo taken when they returned later in the summer, on their way to Georgia. After a short visit to the headquarters, it was time for Gerry and Jane to hike.

The Appalachian Trail Conservancy headquarters are on a blue-blaze trail, as important a side trip off the main trail as there is. Gerry and Jane left the building behind and followed the blazes up Washington Street, due south along Storer College Place, crossing Fillmore Street, and onto the old Storer College campus. They walked past the iron benches under the pretty old oak trees that line the walkway and used to offer shade to students and faculty nearly 150 years ago. They passed in front of the main building of the college, now the Park Service's Stephen T. Mather Training Center, and followed the blue blazes down some steps beside the Harpers Ferry Center Library. Beyond the short stairway, the blazes lead across another walkway and into the woods. It was a proper trail now, skirting down the ancient riverbanks of the Shenandoah River. A short walk took them to where their blue blaze met the Appalachian Trail.

They were on their way.

Harpers Ferry is one of the few towns the AT cuts directly through. Once they were on the famous AT white blazes, Gerry and Jane followed the trail east and stepped onto Church Street, walking along the edge of the road into downtown. They followed High Street, past old John Brown's Fort, and walked across the Goodloe Byron Memorial footbridge over the Potomac River. The river being the interstate border, they were already in Maryland. They followed the trail east along the Chesapeake and Ohio Canal Towpath, and under the Sandy Hook Road overpass on US Route 340. The trail is gentle as it follows the Potomac. It is a pretty, tree-lined path, but on the far side of Route 340, the trail jumps sharply uphill with sixteen switchbacks, climbing only about nine hundred feet of elevation on their way to the Edward B. Garvey Memorial Shelter. The women were thrilled. The redbuds and the red columbine were blooming, and in April you can smell wild clove that grows next to the trail along the switchbacks. They were living their dream.

Gerry's e-mailed trail log to Betty Anne describes the hike's beginning with her simple, honest, and clean prose:

AT Trail Tale #1

April 23, morning, through April 27, evening. 58.8 miles=11.8 avg per day. Shortest day, 9.6, longest 14.2. Weather chilly in the mornings, low 40's. Days warming up to mid-50's to mid 60's, peeling layers all along.

We met up with my friend, Jane Lee, and her husband, James, on April 22 in Harpers Ferry, WV. We sorted and repacked our gear, ate an early dinner, and left Harpers the next morning. We began at the Appalachian Trail Conservancy office and followed a side street down to the AT. It runs out of town past some wonderful historic buildings. In 0.3 miles, we walked across the Potomac River on an old trestle bridge and landed in MD. We walked along the C&O Canal Towpath for 0.9 miles and turned into the woods. Hiked to Gathland State Park. Lovely memorial to war correspondents, but no camping. Rather than get busted our first night for stealth camping (camping in a non-camping spot), in a state park no less, we drove to Greenbrier State Park, about 10 miles north, and set up a base camp for three nights. This worked great as it rained the second night; we didn't have to worry about setting up or taking down our tents in the rain, and they dried out the next day. We won't always be this lucky, I know. Lovely park, nearly deserted. Our Sherpa (George) shuttled us to the next 2 mornings' departure points . . . and hiked in those afternoons to meet us.

Apr 24. Walked through Washington Monument State Park. Built in 1827, it was the first monument to George W to be completed. Reminds me of an old sugar mill in the Caribbean. Great view from the top. Birder up there counting migrating raptors.

Apr 25. Trail very rocky with one area of large rocks all massed together, maybe 150 yards. A slow go. Only 2 through hikers have passed us. They told us in Harpers that 12 total had come through. Plenty early for thru hikers. Guess this would be a good point to tell you why the heck we began at Harpers Ferry. We needed to begin a little later than the typical March 1–April 15 exodus from Springer Mountain, GA. (This due to a visit to CA to see grand baby #3 after her birth on March 5!) Starting from Harpers serves several purposes: avoidance of mass of hikers beginning at Springer, all needing camping spots, shelter, rides to town, resupply . . . the estimate is that 35 people leave Springer every day for about 45 days; avoidance of the mid-Atlantic states in height of summer when so hot and water dwindles; fun of following spring north; and ascending Mt. Katahdin before snow is an issue. Also, the terrain is fairly easy for a while and you can break yourself in more gradually. We hope to make it to Maine by late July, early August . . . return to Harpers and head south.

Apr 26. Broke camp. George dropped us off at our starting point, and he headed to Gettysburg for the day. From there he would spend the night in Mechanicsburg, PA. Jane and I were packed up to hike overnight. We crossed the Mason Dixon line into PA about noon. Shortly after that, the landscape changed from the beauty of Maryland to an alien forest . . . dried, no understory, 100's of dead trees, both standing and fallen. Seemed like very few of the standing were even budded out. Not so much as a squirrel in sight. No birdsong. We later found out that insects have been the main cause; the emerald ash borer has wiped out the ash, the woolly adelgid has wiped out the hemlocks, and the gypsy moth has done a number on the oaks. Heart-breaking. Spent this night at a fabulous shelter. Actually 2 buildings . . . one for snorers and one for non-snorers! Not a mouse in sight. So clean it was unbelievable. Usually the shelters are vermin heaven. The caretakers stopped by while we were making dinner. Come every day to check on things. Very nice couple. As of tonight, what seemed like a full moon for 4 nights. Gorgeous. And owls hooting as well :). 3 guys showed up shortly before we were headed for sleep. Nice, quiet. Slept in snoring building. Made nice fire in morning . . . offered for us to share it while we drank our coffee.

Apr 27. Highlight was Chimney Rocks with fabulous view to the east. George met us at end of days' trek . . . to hotel for shower, laundry, hot meal, comfy bed! Yay!

Wildlife: 2 pileated woodpeckers, nuthatches (black headed), bluejay, goldfinch, chickadees, rabbits, deer. Squirrel corn, bluets, spring beauties, Jack in the Pulpits, abundant May apples. Plenty others, and me without my book!

A grand beginning!

Hiking can be blissful, and it can be stressful. There are myriad contributing factors to which way a hike will go. Luck, weather, health, attitude—all these things play a part in what we individually get out of a hike. The effects of the factors are exponentially compounded when the hike is long-distance. Over the next two and a half months, Gerry and Jane's adventure went quite well. The system that Gerry and George (and Doyle) had worked out with resupplies and support was working. While hiking the trail, the duo was slow, averaging Gerry's pace—only one mile an hour. But that's not uncommon on the AT. With every hundred miles of progress the two made, anecdotes accumulated. While most days were simply lovely—a special overlook, a moment of trail magic, an exceptional experience of trail culture—there were the inevitable down days, too. There were rainy days and painful days. The two worked together to get through them. Through even the worst days, Gerry often smiled.

Gerry's love of nature and of scholarship was endearing.

"We played a lot of games to pass the time as we walked," recalls Jane. "One was a spelling game where we'd take turns calling out letters. Whoever came up with the word first won. We played them for miles and miles. Gerry won nine out of ten times."

The physical stress of an endurance hike affects the mind. Warren Doyle knows that very well—as do all thru-hikers. Doyle states that the hiker's mind is the most important piece of equipment—that training your brain to handle the variables that will inevitably present themselves on the journey is the key to success. Sometimes the variables can seem like an onslaught. In a good year, expect rain (sometimes snow) on at least 20 percent of the days. On another 20 percent, expect it to be too hot to hike comfortably. Mismanaged zero days—rest days—happen often. Blisters? Almost every hiker gets them. Lost toenails? You bet. I've noticed that young men will occasionally complain that they have to go too long between beer or pizza; yet you never hear women complain about losing skin or toenails or having to deal with feminine issues on the trail. The women almost invariably just tough it out. There is someone from every walk of life on the trail, and 99 percent are a joy to encounter. There are those rare young men who are basically just pricks, and, well, everyone on the AT must deal with them.

For Gerry and Jane, there were the normal difficulties. Also, once the women were well into their hike, Gerry would sometimes get turned around. The fact is that the number of people who get turned around on the trail is remarkable. It's just so easy to do. In search-and-rescue operations, I have been on teams that have navigated through the Wind River Mountains by simple dead reckoning. Still, twice when I stepped off the Appalachian Trail, I became momentarily disoriented. Each time I realized how easy it would be to become truly lost. I was confident that I could survive for many weeks in the forest and would be able to make my way out, but it was disconcerting nevertheless.

There are those hikers in Appalachian Trail lore who are famous for getting lost. Some of them were doing their aimless wandering in the old days when the trail wasn't as nicely defined as it is now. But, I assure you, someone became temporarily turned around last week on the AT (it doesn't matter when you read this). The famous Emma Rowena "Grandma" Gatewood, the first woman to thru-hike the AT by herself, did so relying on the kindness of strangers—mostly for directions. An Ohio farm girl who, at age sixty-seven, wanted to—like Earl Shaffer before her—walk the war out of her system, Emma's war was a bit more private. At age nineteen, she had married a young man who was one of those young pricks who grew up to be an even bigger prick. Within the first year of their marriage, her husband began beating her, and he never stopped. He broke her teeth, as well as her ribs. On at least three occasions, she nearly died. In 1940, the year before first-time thru-hiker Earl Shaffer enlisted in the army, Emma divorced her abusive husband. Ten years later, she read a year-old *National Geographic* article about the Appalachian Trail titled "Skyline Trail from Maine to Georgia." After five years of thinking it over, she decided to walk it. In Keds sneakers. Her shelter was a used shower curtain. She made her "pack" out of denim. In it was a raincoat, the shower curtain, an army surplus blanket, and not much else. In her first attempt to hike the trail starting at Mount Katahdin, Emma became hopelessly lost near Rainbow Lake, just south of Baxter State Park. She was eventually found by a game warden and some park rangers and was flown from Rainbow to Millinocket Lake in a Warden Service seaplane. Her first attempt was certainly a disaster, but she tried again, and despite getting lost several more times, she made it and became famous along the way. She became the model for successful hiking through sheer determination.

Jane Lee noticed that Gerry became disoriented more than a few times when starting out the morning's hike. When she pointed it out, Gerry would become frustrated. Despite this, the hike was going well.

By early June, Jane and Gerry were enjoying themselves immensely. They were up to the task. George was settled into his groove and helping along the way, and the weather was cooperating. On June 5, having just crossed the Housatonic River in Massachusetts, moving along at Gerry's slow but deliberate pace, they met seventy-two-year-old Mary Blanton—trail name *Tenderfoot*—from Vermont who was section hiking on her third complete Appalachian Trail hike. Somewhere between the Hemlocks Shelter and the Tom Leonard Lean-To, Mary, the longtime veteran of the AT and experienced hiker, was having a lunch break. Gerry and Jane stopped and chatted for a time—long enough for Mary to learn that the two hikers were attempting a flip-flop from Harpers Ferry. Four days later, about a mile from the summit of Mount Greylock, the three met up again.

Gerry and Jane were poking along, hiking and chatting with several other women as *Tenderfoot* passed them. Mary was a faster hiker. It was a warm, sunny, bluebird day. Mary lingered on the summit, having lunch and enjoying the spring day—the dark green lowlands stretching below her, punctuated by lighter green fields of spring hay and by the overgrown meadows of run-out farms of yesteryear. On her way down from the summit, Mary overtook Gerry and Jane once more, and the women walked and talked on their way to Massachusetts Route 2, where George was waiting for them. The Appalachian Trail has a way of making acquaintances, even lifelong friends, out of random hikers.

"They gave me a ride to my motel, which was nice of them," Mary remembers. "I got a late start in the morning, as I had to shop for some food and had a mail drop to do. So, I didn't see them on the trail, but when I got to Congdon Shelter, they were already there."

That night, it rained hard, and it would only stop intermittently for the next three weeks.

Mary recalls, "Jane had an umbrella, which impressed me no end, as I had never seen a hiker carry a lightweight umbrella. It came in handy on that night! I shared some information with Gerry about the trail between Congdon Camp and Stratton Pond. They were pushing through to Manchester, as there are no access roads for George to meet them."

According to her journal, *Tenderfoot* left the shelter before Gerry and Jane. Four days later, Mary met George at Mad Tom Notch—the first gap in the trail past Manchester.

"We chatted for a while," Mary remembers, "and I gave him my phone number. I invited the three to spend a few nights with me for some zero days when they got to Vermont. George is such a lovely and gentle person. I was glad I met him there; I thought I would see the ladies by Manchester, but he gave me information about their progress—Gerry and Jane had spent an extra night on the trail to complete that section. They weren't fast hikers at that point. Gerry had mentioned a history of a bad back, so I'm sure they were simply taking their time, and Jane was maintaining whatever pace Gerry set."

Gerry, Jane, and George did visit Mary at her home and spent several nights. "It was so lovely having them," recalls Mary. "We talked at length about why we hike, and I remember several fine supper conversations. I thought it was interesting that they had sold their house in Georgia, packed up their belongings, and planned to move back to the Nashville area after the AT to be closer to their grandchildren. They were upbeat and friendly. I loved having them there."

When the group disbanded, George, Gerry, and Jane continued north into New Hampshire, and Mary, a month later, would be off to Mount Katahdin to hike the section south, all the way back to Vermont.

In July, I'll run into them again in the Hundred-Mile Wilderness, Mary thought.

Much of June that year was miserable. Eleven inches of rain fell over Connecticut, Massachusetts, and Vermont. Hikers could not dry out their gear or their feet. In New Hampshire, the White Mountains became more difficult because of the wet terrain. The countless dripping springs that normally slither down the rocks and steep hillsides, cooling the air in the summertime, became torrents that tore down the steep trails.

On June 29, Jane Lee, who is also a nurse, received a call that her grown daughter, while herself hiking, had fractured her ankle. It was an injury that required extra care. Jane would have to return home. It was tough news for Gerry, and for George. *Inchworm* had lost her companion.

Now there was a dilemma: None of Gerry's close friends had wanted her to attempt the Appalachian Trail alone, *but* George's support and supply system had been working well (and would continue to do so). Both husband and wife were aware of the physical demands posed by the trail in New Hampshire's White Mountains. They knew she would have to negotiate the tough Maine section soon. George also knew that Gerry had a fear of the dark and was anxious about being alone. After careful consideration, George and his wife of forty-two years agreed to keep going. Gerry and Jane became teary-eyed when they parted ways and agreed to keep in touch through e-mails as Gerry continued her hike.

Inchworm, moving slower than ever through the difficult White Mountains—referred to by hikers as "the Whites"—carried on.

Other hikers were feeling the wrath of the rain. Father-and-son hiking team Bobby *Kermit* Thompson (age thirty) and Lee *Newton* Thompson (age sixty) were struggling by the end of June. They had started their northbound flip-flop hike on the New York–Connecticut border on June 1.

"The month of June was miserable," recalls Bobby. "It felt like it rained every day through Connecticut, Mass, and Vermont. We could barely dry out our gear or our feet after walking through mud and knee-deep water." *Kermit* remembers one day cursing the sky and wondering what the hell he was doing this for. "This wasn't what Dad and I signed up for," he said.

Hiking not far from *Kermit* and *Newton* was a fifty-seven-year-old seasoned hiker named Terry *Blue Moon* Bliss. From Cooperstown, New York, *Blue Moon* was a traditional thru-hiker and was crushing it. Terry Bliss is tall and lanky and, like so many men thru-hiking the AT, sported a scraggly beard while on the trail. He's gregarious and, like Gerry, loves learning about new things and meeting new people.

Late in June, after a particularly gruelling day scrambling up water-falls, *Kermit, Newton,* and *Blue Moon* met at the Galehead Hut, where they did some light work in exchange for sleeping in the hut and for food. Bliss had to set mousetraps and sweep the floors. All the wet weather also disheartened him, but he offered encouragement to the father and son. They listened intently to *Blue Moon* recount his experiences in the southern portion of the trail, which *Kermit* and *Newton* had yet to hike. They felt consoled by what they heard. The next day, the sun finally came out. *Kermit* was uplifted. The three parted ways for the time being, but father and son and *Blue Moon* would hike together off and on throughout the rest of the summer.

Gerry's first solo night on the trail was at Eliza Brook Shelter. It couldn't have gone better for her. Terry Bliss was there.

The shelter was quite new—less than three years old. Gerry set up on the far left side of the shelter; Terry was on the right. They both remarked on how nice it was that the clean, yellowing log walls were quite free of graffiti. The two hikers shared stories about family members back home and wondered what it was that had attracted them to take such a long hike. Gerry mentioned that her family had concerns about her "midlife escape" but were very supportive. She explained how George was meeting her every few days to take her from the trail for some rest. "We call him *Sherpa*," said Gerry. At one point, Terry saw her sprinkle Gold Bond powder onto her feet, which she did daily. "You're the only person I've seen on the trail other than me using foot powder," said Terry. "I think people know when I've been around from the sprinkles of powder on the ground near the edge of the shelters." Before they turned in, Terry told *Inchworm* about his online hiking blog.

The next day, Gerry was up before Terry, and, after saying goodbye, she left. She did not sign the shelter logbook, and it was her habit not to. Terry remembers, "She looked spry, happy, and she took off with ease and assuredness. She looked like a confident, experienced backpacker." Gerry, while not a powerhouse hiker, would make a habit of inspiring other hikers and endearing people to her along the way. She did so by her unassuming manner and overcoming her trepidations.

Terry left the shelter some time afterward. "I didn't see *Inchworm* on the trail again that day," recalls Terry. Gerry had a habit of having a Carnation Instant Breakfast when she woke up and then hitting the trail. She would usually stop about three hours later, take a break, have something more to eat, and typically find a place to "use the bathroom." That had become her routine. Perhaps she was doing just that when Terry hiked by. Later in the day, Terry stepped out of the woods and into a clearing that serves as an AT parking lot for the Flume Visitor Center. It was only nine miles from the previous night's shelter. A man called out to him, "Are you *Blue Moon*?" It was George. Gerry had texted him that she had met Terry the night before. *Blue Moon* introduced himself. Terry explained that he expected a couple of mail drops at the visitor's center. George then offered to drive Terry the mile to the center. When they returned to the trail, *Inchworm* still hadn't shown. George gave Terry his phone number so he could call him in the future if he needed any more help with the remainder of his hike. George spread his own trail magic along the way, making the most of the adventure. It would be the only time Terry ever saw George.

On July 3, *Blue Moon*, *Kermit*, and *Newton* met up once again at the well-known Zealand Falls Hut at 1:00 p.m. *Kermit* rejoiced when the sun came out again for the first time since they had seen each other the previous week. *Kermit* drew a smiling sun in his journal. It became a beautiful day, the mud drying in the warmth of the early summer sun. *Kermit*—Bobby—and his dad purchased some soup and bread in the kitchen and made their way to the sunny front porch. There *Blue Moon* introduced them to *Inchworm*. Gerry told the men that she had stayed at the hut the previous night. She told *Kermit* that she was taking it slow—slower than her normal pace—through the Whites because of the awful terrain and the appalling, persistent rain. "I'm seriously considering giving up the hike," Gerry told Bobby. "The trail just doesn't seem to be possible with so much rain."

So much can be made bearable by spending time in nature, by simply cherishing the wild beauty in front of you. With the sun beating down on them after so many rainy days, *Kermit* told her one of his favorite quotations he had heard from a thru-hiker the week before: "Happiness is solar-powered."

"Oh, I like that," said Gerry. "I'm going to put it in my journal."

Kermit encouraged her to keep going. "This rain can't last forever," he told her. He was correct: July and August were much sunnier.

Gerry wrote in her journal:

July 5, morning, through July 9, evening. 26.4 miles=6.6 avg per day. Shortest day, 4.8, longest 7.8. 847.5 miles down, 319 to Mt. Katahdin, plus the 20 I have to make up. Low 50's to upper 70's. Mostly cloud cover, fog, mist, some rare sunshine.

I began my three-night hut tour on July 5th. On that day, I hiked only 6.4 miles to my first hut, Mizpah. The rock ascents and descents reminded me of the photo I sent of the PA cliff. At dinner that night (dinner served family style), I met a wonderful family of twelve and that wasn't even the whole clan . . . it was just those who could come. Liz and Jim, the grandma and grandpa; 3 daughters plus one of their husbands; and 6 grandsons, ages 8–13. There were some hardcore hikers in the bunch. Tina and Matt had hiked 2 months in the Yukon on their honeymoon. I spent a delightful evening chatting with many in the fam. As luck would have it, the next morning as everyone was preparing to leave, Jim asked me to hike with him as everyone else leaves him in the dust . . . he said. He was a fine hiking partner. We were climbing from 3800 feet to 5100 feet over 4.8 miles. We passed turn-offs for 8 4000 foot plus summits. There are people called "peak baggers" who climb and keep track of how many 4000 footers they have summited. There are 48 such summits in NH. We ended the day at the next hut, Lake of the Clouds. It was socked in, just like the whole hike had been. However, after dinner, the clouds began to break apart, and we could actually see a bit of sunset. My roommates that night were a French family from eastern Canada. Many visitors to the White Mountains come from there. The dad was fairly fluent, the mom not so much, and their 3 sons, barely. But we had a good time exchanging some limited vocabulary.

*The following day, July 7, Jim was my hiking partner once again.
We started the hike by summiting Mt. Washington. It was a 1.5-
mile hike from the hut, and the ascent was not terribly difficult. Its
elevation is 6288 feet and it boasts the worst weather in the world.
In 1934, a record wind of 231mph was recorded. On this day, the
mountain was fogged in; temp 52, average wind speed of 46, gusting
to 69. Anyone who has read "A Walk in the Woods" may remember that
this mountain is where Bill Bryson learned about killer cotton. By
the time we reached the top, the fog cleared a little and we had some
limited, quick views. We visited the small museum and historic hotel
at the top, met up with some more of the family, then continued on.
The trail to our final hut, Madison, was another 6.2 miles, all above
tree line with a strong wind; it crossed numerous talus fields (acres of
fragmented rock . . . see Wikipedia) and boulders. I think I may have
mentioned rock cairns before; piles of stones that mark the way across
the treeless summits. Interesting to note that often a large piece of
milky quartz is at the top; it is so much easier to see in the mist than
the brown stones.*

*July 8. A tough go. Rained all day. Began with a climb to the
summit of Mt. Madison, from 4800 feet to 5366. From there, we
descended to 2300 feet. It took nearly 6 hours to do the first 3 miles . . .
10 of us including the 6 kids. Then 4 hours for the remaining 5 miles,
although everyone but me was able to stop 2 miles short at a road
crossing. I pushed on the final 2 miles to be completely honest about
my mileage :) and mercifully it was level and I was able to move fast.
It was another one of those days wading the trail. Those kids were
real troopers. Hated to say good bye to the whole family at the end of
the day. They made many, many miles in the White Mountains pass
quickly, and I welcomed the company.*

*A word about the huts . . . there are 8 in the White Mountains,
most roughly a day's hike apart. The bunk rooms are coed, dinner
served at 6PM and breakfast at 7AM. There are composting priv-
ies (not nearly as odiferous as the usual outhouse) and cold running
tap water in the bathrooms. You are provided with a pillow and 3
woolen blankets. You bring your own sheets or sleeping bag. Lights out*

at 9:30. The staff sings you awake at 6:30. The staff consists of hard working college kids who are delightful. Loved the experience.

Sherpa stays in town while I am gone; he seems more than content to do so and often walks in to meet me on the final day. The motels we are staying in are mostly circa 50's and 60's . . . think the Griswold's family vacation! Flowered wallpaper, linoleum in the bath, white ruffled curtains (maybe not so recently laundered); one even had the old "Magic Fingers" coin box on the wall! But they have all been clean, with clean sheets and towels . . . and they don't smell like cigarette smoke. Makes me think of the road trips we took back in the day long before the interstates went everywhere.

The wet, miserable deluges of June were over. It wouldn't rain hard again until July 22, when Gerry would step off the trail and find herself in yet a different state of mind.

Then everything would change.

Chapter Four

Maine

What would life be if we had no courage to attempt anything?
—Vincent van Gogh

The Appalachian Trail seems to be peopled with giving individuals. There are very few profligates (if indeed there are any). Dottie *.Com* Rust is an educator who has spent years teaching the deaf. Tim *Walker* McElhannon spent a career serving his country. Regina *Queen* Clark, like Gerry Largay and Jane Lee, is a registered nurse. George Largay had served in the air force and was involved in his church. They are all giving people. Gerry's friends repeatedly recount that she was giving of her time, her attention, and her love. Perhaps that is what people who met her on the trail sensed about her. Maybe it was her ready smile that put people at ease.

On July 21, at the same time *Inchworm*, George, and Tim were saying their final, awkward goodbyes in the middle of the trail on their way north toward Poplar Ridge Lean-To, two extraordinary women were picking their way south from Mount Katahdin: Dottie *.Com* Rust and Regina *Queen* Clark—both from Maryland. Both women were section hikers, nearing their goal of hiking the entire Appalachian Trail. They were fit, seasoned hikers in their fifties. They hoped to knock off the entire state of Maine on this trip.

Dottie and Regina had started their hike on July 2, summiting Katahdin in three hours. At Rainbow Lake, where Grandma Gatewood had become lost fifty-eight years earlier, the two hikers met another section hiker who was having a difficult time. He was very dehydrated. Registered nurse Regina, always a caregiver, gave the parched man some electrolyte tablets. He was moving so slowly that the women thought he might be on the trail more days than he had expected, so they shared with him some of their carefully planned-out food.

You could call it trail magic on the hoof.

Four days later, the two seasoned hikers, after tenting near Cooper Brook in the Hundred-Mile Wilderness, had trouble finding white blazes on the trail and lost nearly a half hour of hiking time. On July 9, on their way to Long Pond Stream Lean-To, Regina and Dottie met a hiker from West Virginia called *M-Dot*. His hiking partner, *Ned the Fed*, had had an accident ascending Katahdin eight days earlier. Maine Association for Search and Rescue sent a helicopter to transport him to a Bangor hospital after a boulder had fallen on him, dislocating his shoulder and crushing his foot. The Appalachian Trail isn't for the faint of heart. Like most people, after finishing the Hundred-Mile Wilderness, *.Com* and *Queen* took a zero day, lounging at the celebrated Shaw's Hiker Hostel in Monson and feasting on Shaw's famous breakfast of lots of coffee, pancakes, eggs, bacon, sausage, and juice. The two friends were having an epic hike.

While Gerry inched her way north to Poplar Ridge Lean-To, Regina and Dottie hiked south from their tent sites on the Carrabassett River to the same shelter. It would be a rough walk. Fourteen miles from the river to Poplar Ridge meant eleven hours on the rough trail for Dottie and Regina. Tired, dirty, and anxious to get to the shelter, the women were focused and working hard on the trail. The terrain was steep and difficult, and the forests were thick. About five hundred feet below the summit of Poplar Ridge, the two women stepped over a plank footbridge that crossed a small spring. The forest here is mostly beech and oak, with the odd birch tree. It was open and pretty. The forest floor was littered with beechnut shells and acorns cracked open by the deer and the squirrels. Beyond the spring, the trail makes a quick ascent, requiring hikers to scramble up steep granite slabs, where the beech and oak give way first to tamaracks and then to balsams. As the two women climbed higher, they passed the steep granite slabs to find themselves amid the scraggly spruce, scrub juniper, and fir trees. The forest became so thick it was nearly impenetrable.

Breaking the pace and the silence, Regina stopped, peered into the woods, and said, "God, if you were six feet off the trail, you'd be a goner! Can't see anything in there." Dottie replied, "Good for you—now you see why I keep asking if you 'have a white blaze.'"

They had made an early start and finished in good time, arriving at the shelter at 4:30 in the afternoon. Dottie and Regina walked up to the shelter, finally able to slide off their packs. Two women were already there—a quiet woman who had set up her tent away from the shelter and Gerry Largay. As is the custom, they initially introduced themselves by their trail names. Regina, Dottie, and Gerry—*Queen*, *.Com*, and *Inchworm*—hit it off immediately.

Gerry told the newcomers, "And this is *Ivanich*. She's a thru-hiker. She doesn't say much."

Indeed, *Ivanich* didn't say much.

Dottie remembers being touched. "*Inchworm* was gracious in the way she made the laconic *Ivanich* feel included." Gerry had met *Ivanich* occasionally along the trail, but they hadn't hiked together. Dottie and Regina were drawn to the sixty-six-year-old Gerry, and the three talked until they were all too tired to stay up any longer. *Queen* and *.Com* set up their tent near the small spring that runs next to the shelter. There were other tents across the spring, away from the campsite. Two young boys had an open tarp set up next to the shelter.

Regina and Gerry talked about their field of nursing—how much it has changed and how lately money (insurance and hospital revenue) and politics had become at least as important as patient care. They worried that changes in the medical field in the last decade, such as the absurd amount of documentation required, have greatly impacted a nurse's ability to provide tender loving care. They talked about their families. Gerry told both Regina and Dottie that her hiking partner had been called away and that she planned on finishing alone with the help of her husband. They talked about gear, as all AT hikers love to do. (Except perhaps *Ivanich*.) The three women were all using the same make and model backpack: ULA's Circuit.

Gerry told Dottie how she preferred sleeping in a lean-to rather than her tent and that she "didn't at all like the dark at night."

Dottie replied, "Yeah, when the lights go off out here, it's truly dark."

After supper and two hours of talking and getting to know one another, all three women lay down in their sleeping bags for a much-needed rest. The sun went down, the headlights went out, and it was very dark. But Gerry was not in her tent. She was in the shelter, and she was not alone.

Regina and Dottie were up in the morning at 5:30. Gerry was also awake early, as usual. She organized her gear and had her instant breakfast. Regina and Dottie were getting their gear ready as well. Gerry would be heading north, alone, to the Spaulding Mountain Lean-To. Dottie and Regina would again be southbound. At 7:26, Gerry texted George to let him know she was leaving the Poplar Ridge Lean-To: *About to leave shelter. Don't worry about getting stuff for 100 Mile Wilderness.* (She wouldn't hike the Hundred-Mile Wilderness for several days yet.) After a second night on the trail—at the Spaulding Mountain Lean-To—she would meet George where the AT crosses Route 27 in Wyman Township.

After their enjoyable night together, talking and getting to know one another, southbound hikers Regina and Dottie were sad to part ways with *Inchworm.* As Gerry shouldered her pack, Dottie asked if she could take her picture. "It would make a great Christmas card," said Dottie.

"Of course!" Gerry laughed.

Gerry cut quite a figure in her beige hiking shorts, her red fleece sweater, gaiters over her ankles to keep the ticks at bay, her kerchief covering her hair, and the emergency whistle dangling from her pack strap. She looked tanned and fit. She was the picture of health and happiness.

Dottie readied her camera, and said, "I want to be *Inchworm* when I grow up!" Gerry smiled as she buckled her pack belt. Dottie snapped the photo. Gerry turned and headed up the trail.

It was the last verbal exchange Gerry Largay had on Earth.

In the words passed between them was an inspiration for Regina and Dottie that will last forever.

CHAPTER FIVE

Off the Beaten Path

As the Trail in Maine leads through an utter wilderness, often dis-
tant many days' journey from the nearest town or road, admittedly to
become lost from the Trail in Maine would be a serious matter. But let
no one, who would otherwise undertake this journey, be deterred by
any such consideration for those responsible for the Trail have devoted
much emphasis to its marking.

—MYRON AVERY, 1937

Reading Avery's words, one's mind might turn to the amazing people who keep the Appalachian Trail alive—the maintainers, ridgerunners, and volunteers. It's a fact: Nobody knows sections of the AT more intimately than the trail maintainers. They become familiar with every rock, root, and trickle of water on their section. They know where the spring runoff is most likely to damage the trail. They know the spots that might pose the most difficulty for hikers. They know where the best rest stops are (not to mention the best views). They know where there's cell service—and where cell phones are useless. They know the places where the unyielding black-flies will be worse and, after them, the mosquitos. They know the corridors on both sides of the trail like the backs of their hands.

When Gerry Largay swung down the path from the Poplar Ridge Lean-To on her way to Orbeton Stream (almost entirely downhill), the trail she was hiking had for half a century been maintained by forester, professor, and one-time Maine Appalachian Trail Club president David Field. For thirty-eight years, beginning in 1957, David had maintained more than seven miles of the trail from the summit of Saddleback Mountain to Orbeton Stream. For the first seven of those years, he enlisted help from his brother and friends. But by 1995, he had reduced his assignment area, to stop trail maintenance at the top of the Horn—a mile short of Saddleback. The University of Maine professor returned each year, clearing blowdowns and brush, painting blazes, building bog bridges, and caring for the Poplar Ridge Lean-To. He walked and understood the corridor boundaries. David had grown up in Madrid, Maine, in the shadow of the Appalachian Trail that would become a force in his life. In 2015, David gave up the trail-maintenance assignment after fifty-nine years.

Some years ago, during an AT reroute of 5.7 miles that would include Lone Mountain, David designed the new section of the trail from Orbeton Stream to near Spaulding Mountain. Nobody alive knows the section of the Appalachian Trail from Poplar Ridge to the Spaulding Mountain Lean-To better than Dr. David Field.

Gerry, living up to her trail name, carefully poked her way to Orbeton Stream, 1,500 feet in elevation below the Poplar Ridge Lean-To. Much of the trail on the north side of Poplar Ridge below the summit is a steep descent. Gerry's one-mile-per-hour pace is not unreasonable for that section. *Inchworm* scooted, slid, and picked her way down the same steep, smooth, granite slabs that Dottie and Regina had climbed up the day before. She made her way through the oak, beech, and birch woods. She walked across the plank bridge over the little spring. As she made her way to Orbeton Stream, she stepped across the large, flat rocks in parts of the trail, placed there strategically in boggy spots years ago—perhaps decades ago—by David Field. Around ten in the morning, she reached Orbeton Stream, picking her way across, stepping from boulder to boulder. It's a ford; it can't be crossed with dry feet. Once on the far side, she clambered up the steep, hundred-foot climb to where the trail crosses a wide path. But this is no tote road—a pathway cut into the woods in the old days, wide enough for the horses to twitch out logs. This path in the woods is more defined: it is the ancient bed of the narrow-gauge Phillips and Rangeley Railroad, later named the Sandy River and Rangeley Lakes Railroad and referred to by locals as "the Sandy River Line." The steel tracks are long gone now. Today it's just an easy trail through the woods, passable with ATVs and mountain bikes. The alliterative Railroad Road is a well-known landmark to locals.

Once Appalachian Trail hikers reach the top of the steep scramble up from Orbeton Stream to Railroad Road, there is a nice set of rocks to sit on where the Appalachian Trail continues. It's very likely Gerry sat there, on the side of old Railroad Road, and rested. Most hikers do. Sitting on the rocks, if one looks to the east, the "road" trundles down a valley along Orbeton Stream to the village of East Madrid, less than a day's walk, where Perham Stream cuts through farmsteads dating to the 1700s.

To the west of the Railroad Road rest stop, the road travels steadily "upgrade," as the old railroad men used to say, through the conifer forests lined with maples, white and yellow birches, and a few oak trees. The railroad bed crosses over four tiny brooks that drain the hills to the north on their way to Orbeton Stream. Mainers call them "feeder brooks." The road continues on to the abandoned Redington Township on the shores of Redington Pond, where the steam locomotives would stop for water and the passengers from New York and Pennsylvania would stretch their legs.

Once one of the best native brook trout waters in Maine, long ago Redington Pond was one of the destinations where guides would bring their "sports" to fish and have cocktails. There was a railroad depot on the shoreline. Today, the ghost town, the pond, and thousands of surrounding acres are owned by the United States Navy, where it conducts its training in Survival, Evasion, Resistance, and Escape (SERE) school.

That Gerry had gone missing on a part of the AT adjacent to a top-secret navy institution was of more than passing interest to some people. (But not to any of the people searching for her.) Some people even suggested that the presence of the navy survival school may have explained why Gerry went missing to begin with. Before being drawn into that conspiracy theory, it's important to realize what the SERE program is and what it attempts to accomplish.

The SERE program is an advanced code-of-conduct course. All military personnel get their initial code-of-conduct instruction during basic training, in which they are taught an American service member's moral and legal responsibilities if captured by enemy forces. But SERE goes way beyond that. Essentially, the school teaches students how to evade capture and to live off the land and what to do—and *not* do—if captured.

Senior Chief Dennis Haug—a retired multitour SERE instructor assigned to Fleet Aviation Specialized Operational Training Group, Brunswick, Maine—taught individuals what to do when things go from bad to worse. Haug says, "The students who took the course were there to learn how to stay alive *and* the values behind the code of conduct. When the situation is real, the threat is real, so the students need to be ready to handle it."

The instruction begins with a week of classroom work focusing on wilderness survival and real-world applications of the code of conduct for a service member. The program includes an extensive look into ways of surviving off the land. What may sound like a Boy Scout manual—fire building, trapping, creating shelters, finding edible plants—are skills worth having. Haug adds, "Once we have the students on the mountain, we split them into teams and immediately get their hands dirty. Like ducks out of water, they do their best to demonstrate all that we teach them about survival. We teach primitive means of making due with what is at arm's reach, such as constructing a fire with flint and steel, what's edible, and how to use a simple piece of metal as a compass." Everything SERE students learn in the field phase of training prepares them for the simulated "problem." At some point in the training, the problem arises: They are on their own and being pursued by the "enemy." There will be no help from instructors during this phase, and what the students have learned will become the key to their survival. From the minute the students lay their packs under a raggedy silk canopy, which simulates a downed pilot's parachute, they do all they can to become one with nature.

Although the course can be a difficult experience, according to Haug, who grew up in the outdoors hunting, fishing, and camping, "It is a necessary episode. The students never forget the simulations and lessons that are taught," he says. "I would rather see the students screw up in camp, where we can teach proper procedures during a debriefing."

I have interviewed seven retired navy officers who were SERE students. Each one agreed that the course made them more confident in their abilities.

"During the problem phase of the training," says Haug, "the students are expected to work together. Navigation skills will be put to the test, along with rigorous hiking on unknown soil, up and down mountains. Here they use all means necessary for immediate survival, such as making small shelters out of their ponchos." The students gain the technical knowledge, practical experience, and personal confidence necessary for worldwide survival and evasion. No two students are the same, and sometimes individuals find themselves out of their element. Haug says, "There were many students in the courses that had spent all their lives on paved streets, and the only trees they have ever seen grew on street corners."

Knowing how to handle unique individuals is up to the instructors, who are men and women of many parts—naturalists, guides, psychologists, and mentors. Haug is a highly motivated and well-trained fellow and profoundly knowledgeable about survival and search-and-rescue efforts. For years, he was one of few state certifiers for search-and-rescue team leaders. He has experience searching for many lost hikers who were eventually found on the navy's SERE property. "Some years, we found three or four hikers wandering around where they shouldn't be," he says.

The navy has its own search-and-rescue teams called DBAPs—which stands for (officially) *Don't Be a Problem.* They top the alphabetical list of volunteer organizations on the Maine Association for Search and Rescue website. But you won't find their picture, and you won't find much literature about them. They just show up to help the Warden Service when called and then fade away after the search. It is all very separate from the SERE school.

"The course can be tough," says Haug. "And witnessing a student's transition is inspiring and a strong example of human willpower, despite adversity." Haug makes no bones about it: "The strain is . . . abundant." He flattens his hand in the air at chest level. "The stress level at basic training is here. At the SERE school, it's here . . ." (his hand raises above his head).

It's human nature to do all that is necessary to stay alive. The training that takes place in the remote mountains of Maine opens the window into how to survive when things go south. The instructors at SERE have many combined years of knowledge and experience directly from surviving prisoners of war, making this course an invaluable tool for all those who run the risk of capture by enemy forces.

The man in charge of the SERE school and operations in 2013 was Lieutenant Commander J. D. Walker. As a navy pilot, he had been through the program years before taking command of the school. He, more than most, understands the importance of the training and education presented at the SERE school. "As far as the survival part of the program is concerned, the training isn't meant to make attendees experts," says Commander Walker. "It's more of an inoculation. Its design is to give the students a quick exposure—to give them basic skill sets that they can learn and carry with them. If they were to become downed behind enemy lines, it would give them something to hold on to in potentially dire circumstances. God willing, they will hold fast and come out okay."

Between Orbeton Stream and the Spaulding Mountain Lean-To, the southeastern border of the SERE property parallels the Appalachian Trail corridor for more than a mile. Knowing the property well, the navy doesn't conduct many operations close to the AT—but the boundary line along the corridor is there. It's restricted property but not exactly patrolled, though it is "monitored." The property is clearly marked on some maps, totally absent on others. Like all military properties, it's as though the government has drawn a line in the sand.

If Gerry did sit and rest on the rocks on Railroad Road above Orbeton Stream, like so many hikers before her, she didn't linger. Maintaining her usual one-mile-per-hour pace, she turned onto the trail where it follows tiny Sluice Brook upstream. For nearly a half mile, the AT parallels close to the brook through a mixed hardwood forest. The woods are more open there, with beech, maples, and the occasional birch shading the trail. As Gerry hiked this section of trail northbound, the SERE land is to the left, and down the mountain to the right are the ancient farming hamlets and homesteads of East Madrid.

Gerry continued along the trail as it follows up Sluice Brook. The trail is appointed with worked granite steps and carefully laid boulders—some placed there by David Field and his crew years before when he had designed, built, and maintained this section. The boulders are worn smooth, polished first by glaciers and then by decades of shoe leather.

For the next mile, the trail is not difficult. The deciduous trees cast long, thin shadows and offer shade to ferns and the light foliage of the undergrowth. The trail and its protected corridor travel through land that has been forested several times dating back more than one hundred years. Small sections were logged before the Civil War. David Field, who wrote *Along Maine's Appalachian Trail* (2011), can tell you about Calvin Putnam of Danvers, Massachusetts, and Henry Closson, who purchased Redington Township in 1883. Closson had the Phillips and Rangeley Railroad built, which would later be included in the Sandy River Line. They were sitting on twenty-five *million* board feet of old-growth spruce timber in the area. Putnam was the driving force behind building the railroad, which he saw as a great way to get the lumber out of the rugged wilderness. After the old-growth timber was completely removed, the railroad was abandoned in the early 1930s. Logging around Redington continued for pulp and birch used for toothpick, spool, and other specialty wood products. David notes, "The area has a very rich history. Logging continued up there through the 1960s."

"The US Navy acquired more than twelve thousand acres of the township in 1962 and was in the process of building the SERE training camp," says David, "when in June an 1,800-acre forest fire broke out in the Redington Pond Range. The fire was intense in the new slash from recent cutting and burned most of the soil. You can still see the outline of the burn from Saddleback." In *Along Maine's Appalachian Trail*, there is a photograph of the fire in progress.

Now just a pretty path in the woods above Orbeton Stream, Railroad Road is a popular rest stop and "stealth camping" spot for Appalachian Trail thru-hikers.

Gerry hiked on, paralleling Sluice Brook until the trail crosses over the tiny creek, just under a mile from Railroad Road. In that vicinity, sometime between 10 and 11 a.m., Gerry felt the call of nature. The woods are open there, mostly ash and maple, with other varieties of shrubs and shorter trees. Perhaps a little too open for a woman seeking privacy. Hiking alone, she had no one to stand guard for her.

Gerry turned left off the trail, searching for a tree to hide behind. The Appalachian Trail Conservancy (ATC) has guidelines for going to the bathroom in the woods, and for good reason. Hiking the AT is so enjoyable in great part because just about every hiker follows the suggestions. The ATC recommends going at least two hundred feet—or eighty paces—away from water, trails, or shelters. Use a stick to mix dirt with your waste, which hastens decomposition and discourages animals from digging it up. Used toilet paper should either be buried in a cathole dug six to eight inches deep with a plastic trowel, a tent stake, or a dead stick or be carried out in a sealed plastic bag.

Eighty paces to go to the bathroom: According to Jane Lee, when they hiked together Gerry never walked more than about a hundred feet off the trail, staying within sight of Jane as her friend waited. They would often stand watch for each other, keeping an eye on the trail for other hikers. But Gerry was alone now. One hundred feet off the trail . . . as Regina *Queen* Clark had remarked only two days earlier, "Six feet off the trail, and you'd be a goner."

The fact that the woods of Maine are largely thick and overgrown, choked with spruce and fir trees, and difficult to walk through is true enough, but any notion that the open, deciduous forests are easier to negotiate is often an illusion. There's all manner of shrubbery underfoot, and if you walk far enough in the open woods, you'll eventually hit cedars and hackmatack trees, where even in drought years your hiking shoes will get wet and covered with mud.

On the section of trail where Gerry stepped off, she could see quite far into the woods—maybe seventy-five yards. She had to work to get any distance from the well-worn trail. The forest floor there is covered with witch hobble. Also called hobblebush, this shrub, *Viburnum lantanoides*, can grow six to twelve feet high, though where Gerry left the trail it is only three feet tall at the most. The pendulous branches take root where they touch the ground. The intermingled branches, anchored at both ends, form annoying obstacles that can trip or hobble walkers, surveyors, and witches as they run through the woods at night.

Gerry made her way through the trees to a spot out of sight. She worked through the bothersome, entwined witch hobble, past beech, red spruce, and alders until she couldn't be seen from the trail. She knew where the path was; she knew the direction back from where she came. She found a secluded spot.

Everyone who spent time with Gerry tells of her love of nature. She appreciated plants and trees, and especially the birds in the sky. One day, she got excited when she found some lady's slippers. On another, she was thrilled to find a cluster of strange, interesting mushrooms. Songbirds always held her attention.

Once Gerry reshouldered her pack, she took a few steps back toward the Appalachian Trail—or so she thought. She may have been distracted by a particularly attractive flower—there are many in the Redington range. Maybe she saw an uncommon songbird before her first few steps to return to the trail. A lark bunting, perhaps? A redstart? Maybe she wasn't distracted by anything, but her spatial orientation was gone, and it didn't take long for her to realize that she was lost.

It was a scenario familiar to many of us who have been turned around in the forest: *Inchworm* looked around. The trail was not in sight. She tried to get her bearings but could not. She walked for several minutes in what she thought was the correct direction. Then she turned and tried another. Gerry kept walking, hoping to pop out onto the AT. She only switched on her cell phone when she needed to call or text—or if she expected a call from George. It was off now.

Gerry kept trying. Within an hour of realizing that she was lost, she was wandering. In the back of her mind, she knew she was west of the AT. She did have a compass with her—a tiny one, only a half inch in diameter, clipped onto a keychain along with a small thermometer. She had purchased a SPOT Satellite GPS Messenger but didn't have it with her. Gerry had spoken about the SPOT locator weeks earlier while she had been hiking with Dianne *Gummy Bear* Cook. Dianne had offered to help set up the SPOT for her, but Gerry had declined.

The SPOT might be nice to have in the Hundred-Mile Wilderness, but it's not light. *Inchworm* hadn't wanted to carry any weight in her pack that wasn't necessary. Very few thru-hikers bother to carry a SPOT locator. The Appalachian Trail is well marked, after all.

At 11:01 in the morning, Gerry turned on her phone and sent a text to George: *In somm trouble. Got off trail to go to br. Now lost. Can u call AMC to c if a trail maintainer can help me. Somewhere north of woods road. Xox.* (The "woods road" she referred to was Railroad Road, but no one could be sure of that for a very long time.) She looked at the phone: "Message receipt failed." George never got the text.

Inchworm needed to get the message through. She climbed a ridge, hoping for some reception. Nothing. What she didn't know was that she was miles from any cell service.

Gerry often prayed, so she surely prayed then.

CHAPTER SIX

Lost

*Lost in the forest, I broke off a dark twig
and lifted its whisper to my thirsty lips:
maybe it was the voice of the rain crying,
a cracked bell, or a torn heart.*

—PABLO NERUDA

Gerry pushed and thrashed through the thick woods, hoping to find her way, or at least cell phone reception. She apparently felt that even with no cell reception, the higher elevation might make her more visible. Perhaps she might be able to see some landmarks from the heights and get her bearings. Her compass would not help. The size of a suit coat button, it was almost like a toy compass. It might give one a general idea of direction but would be woeful for navigation. She may have tried to use it, but if she did, it's hard to say what her plan was: To the south of where she became lost was Railroad Road (though she didn't know its name, referring to it as a "woods road"), and she knew she was north of that. To the west was the navy's SERE training facility, but she probably did not know where that would be located. To the north was an expanse of forest uninterrupted for miles by any road or structure. Too many miles. To the east was the Appalachian Trail, less than two football fields away. Gerry headed west-southwest, almost paralleling the AT. If her own reckoning was correct about the distance she traveled, she certainly walked in circles for some of her wandering through the woods. Without a map, even using a compass, one needs to know the general direction they *should* be going.

Before she became lost, Gerry had felt purpose in her path and had become a smiling part of the Appalachian Trail community. But now it was primal. Once lost, like so many other lost people before her, she would have no purpose or sense of accomplishment—only desperation. She crossed two brooks and climbed three steep, overgrown ridges. Minimal training in woods craft would have told her to follow either brook downstream. She did not. She tried to get higher. Some of the climbing was hand over fist. The old, half-decayed slash (branches cut from the trees when the forest had been harvested eighty years ago) snagged at her and scratched her legs. She pulled herself through the briar and the brambles. Late in the afternoon, she erected her tent near the second brook. It was an uneven, damp spot, totally invisible from only yards away. It was not a good place. "A crummy spot," she called it in her journal. Once she forded the second brook, Gerry had crossed her Rubicon.

The next day—Tuesday, July 23—it rained hard. At 4:18 in the afternoon, she tried texting her husband again: *Lost since yesterday. Off trail 3 or 4 miles. Call police for what to do pls. Xox.* Again, the text did not go through.

George, waiting at the road crossing, spoke with every hiker he met. Mike *RockSteady* Jurasius, an engineering geologist from California, had hiked twenty-five miles through the torrential rains of the day before and popped out onto Route 27 on July 23. He saw George there.

"Who are you waiting for?" asked Mike.

"My wife," said George. "She's hiking the first half of a flip-flop, and she's supposed to meet me here today." They talked for a while about *Inchworm* and the rain.

"She likely won't make it here until tomorrow," said Mike. Later he recounted, "George offered me a ride into the town of Stratton, but I found another one. He was still there the next day."

On Wednesday, the rain had stopped, and by early afternoon the sun shone. Gerry broke down her tent and moved it to the top of the next ridge. The trees seemed slightly more open there; perhaps she could be seen. It was the highest spot she could reach. She was still only 120 feet from the brook—a good water supply. To keep off the wet ground, she built up a platform of sticks and leaves and erected her tent atop it. She built no hearth.

George, waiting on the side of Route 27, knew the rain might have slowed Gerry down. Weather often causes delays on the Appalachian Trail. Blisters also can eat up an extra day. So can diarrhea. He also had an inkling of how difficult the section of the AT is between Poplar Ridge and where he was waiting. In fact, he and Gerry had talked about how difficult the trail was getting. It's not unusual for hikers to show up a day or two late from a section of the AT. When his wife didn't show up on Wednesday, he didn't panic. Still, he asked every hiker as they emerged from the trail whether they'd seen *Inchworm*.

Nurses typically have the same carriage: alert, yet poised, ever ready to help should the need arise, and to react to a given situation. Gerry, the sixty-six-year-old nurse, tried to stay collected. She figured she would need to ration her two days' worth of food and make a plan. It might be a while before someone found her. She hung up her Mylar space blanket in a relatively open spot thirty yards from her tent, tying the corners of the shiny blanket stretched between branches of alders and young hackmatack trees. She settled in and ate some almonds, a couple of prunes, and some rationed Fritos—approximately three hundred calories for supper—and wrote in her journal. In the waning light of the evening, as darkness descended upon her, she said the rosary. When we are young, faith is a secret that is taught, and when we get older, it is either embraced or not. It is never attained; it is gifted. And, if accepted, faith is like an anchor in a storm and does much to alleviate the mortal fear.

In the wee hours of that Wednesday night, Gerry, lying in her tent, heard only the voice of the tiny brook.

Beyond the normal lost-person behavior, it is impossible to predict how each person may react to being lost, especially with regard to survival or self-rescue. Some stay calm; some tighten with a level of resolve experienced for the first time. Some panic. Most experience a sense of urgency and hurry—hurry to find their way out, to find a high spot, to tie their shoes. Whatever their plan of action is, they often move too fast.

Fear is a powerful emotion. Dr. Ken Hill is a professor of psychology at Saint Mary's University, Halifax, Nova Scotia, Canada, and an expert on lost-person behavior; he says, "Fear stimulates a heightened concern for self-preservation, mobilizing the body for flight through the secretion of adrenalin and increased blood supply to the legs. It's no wonder, therefore, that the lost person's impulse is to move rather than to stay put. Fear can interfere with higher mental functioning, such as concentration and problem solving, and may cause a regression to more 'primitive' modes of thought."

It can be difficult to stay calm when lost in the wilderness. It can take focus and discipline. There are many stories of lost people losing their minds from the stress. I recall a massive search in the 1980s for a hiker who had been lost for only five days in Wyoming's Wind River Mountains. He had bolted from a fisherman who happened upon him on the first day and tried to help him. The lost man apparently kept running for days. When we eventually found his body, it looked like he had run himself to death.

When someone is truly lost, it is instantly traumatic. It affects their behavior. Even if the skills and means are present, few will start fires, perhaps an indicator that they are not accepting their predicament. Or they simply might not have had training in the outdoors. Some don't erect decent shelters, accepting the fact that they are doomed to discomfort. Those who do obtain shelter (Gerry had brought along her backpacking tent) sometimes don't realize how camouflaged it can make them in the forest.

As a lost person moves around in the forest—especially in the "Big Woods," like you find in Maine—it's difficult for them to maintain a good degree of orientation. Without using a compass (and knowing how to use it), they may have the illusion of being oriented—and assume that the way back is in "that" direction merely because the terrain seems to direct them that way.

When someone first realizes they are lost in a forest, they will typically try to reorient themselves. Some will climb a hill or a tree, trying to see a landmark, and some try to backtrack. Some people simply panic. As search-and-rescue communities strive to improve and gain a better understanding of what goes through the mind of a lost person, they should explore the psychology of the victim. Being lost is basically the result of a person losing their spatial orientation—our natural ability to maintain our body orientation in relation to the surrounding environment (our physical space). When we are truly lost, we have lost our spatial orientation, whether we are moving or standing still. When lost, our task is to reorient ourselves. The best way to do that is to carry a compass and know how to use it and to know where you are to begin with—before you get lost—in relation to the cardinal points of the compass (east, south, north, and west). Using the sun will obviously help, but, as we know, sometimes the sun isn't out.

When I was a boy growing up in Maine, my father and uncle taught me what to do if I became lost in the woods. Most all boys and girls were told in those days, unless you lived in a city. Most of the boys I knew then fished and hunted. When my dad and uncle were convinced I'd memorized what they'd taught me, they moved on to survival. First and foremost, they taught me how to use a compass and to never enter the woods without one—*and* without getting a bearing first.

They told me that if I did get lost, I should stay put for as long as I could, and they showed me how to build a shelter. Dad taught me how to start a fire with just the materials around me: with a battery, a bow drill, gunpowder removed from a bullet, with the magnifying glass that was attached to the compass he gave me—to use the sap from a balsam tree as lighter fluid. They said if I were compelled to move—for water, perhaps—then I was to take a proper compass bearing and walk along that line until I found water, and then hunker down again. If the compass was lost or didn't work for some reason, then use the sun to find a course. Hopefully it would be in the general direction back to where I entered the woods. Once I found a brook, however small, I was to follow it downstream. If the brook was "dead water," with no obvious direction of the current, then toss in some dried grass or leaves. Even if it was windy, the debris would eventually go downstream.

I remember my dad standing in front of me with his hand on my shoulder: "A brook becomes a stream, which eventually becomes either a lake or a river. Either way, there'll be roads, or camps, or *something*. You might have to skirt some bogs, but that's okay. Just keep the brook in sight or within hearing distance. You'll get out."

He also told me once, "If a fellow tells you he's a woodsman who's never once been lost, he's either a liar or not a true woodsman at all."

Even that great pathfinder and explorer Daniel Boone is quoted as saying, "I have never been lost, but I will admit to being confused for several weeks."

It's inevitable: Anyone who spends any significant time in the woods—especially in Maine—will become disoriented at some point. Unfortunately, getting lost also happens to those people who are not woodsmen and who enter the woods very rarely. People without training or skills. Every guide worth their salt will tell you they've been "turned around." It's just that they know what to do in such a situation, and they never panic.

In the old days, search-and-rescue personnel were simply told to "put themselves in the lost person's shoes." Coupled with data available that showed statistically how lost people had behaved, rescuers formulated plans. For many decades, the data and the search techniques differed from state to state—even from county to county. Techniques still differ, but it's getting better. There are national and international search-and-rescue organizations and conferences with information sharing, but many states and counties don't participate. Some can't afford to attend. Some simply won't. In my experience, depending on where you are, search-and-rescue communities can be a bit odd. SAR communities, state to state and province to province, are often populated by the same sort of folks: good people bent on helping others. Alas, no matter where you live, professionals in some jurisdictions can be a little turf-oriented.

In Maine, the official search-and-rescue entity is the Maine Warden Service, and Lieutenant Kevin Adam presently heads its SAR department. We Mainers are lucky. We have a world-class fish and wildlife department. The Warden Service search-and-rescue department tries not to be turf-oriented. Lieutenant Adam, a sizable man, has a build tending toward one of a middle-aged man who has stayed very fit because his job requires it. His position as head of the search-and-rescue aspect of the Warden Service appears to be a full-time proposition, but he is still a game warden. When not conducting searches or supervising other wardens, he beats the bush looking for poachers.

Most times, Adam and his staff use every possible avenue to find lost souls, though historically there does seem to be a disconnect between the Warden Service and DEEMI (Downeast Emergency Medicine Institute) Search and Rescue, based out of Orono, Maine. Although both organizations do work together on some rescues, volunteers at DEEMI (as it is known) are left out of others. It might be geographic, and it might be administrative. While the Warden Service routinely uses Maine Association for Search and Rescue–trained volunteer organizations, DEEMI prefers to maintain its certifications through the National Association for Search and Rescue. By doing that, DEEMI can assist the state-funded Marine Patrol, and its members can travel to other states to help in searches without acquiring permission from the Maine Warden Service. DEEMI has an active emergency-room physician on its board, as well as a person trained in psychology. The organization is very medical-based and offers some interesting, innovative ideas about early care for the recovered lost person. I got the sense that some of the DEEMI rescuers felt left out of some rescues because they are not directly controlled by the Warden Service. In some cases, families of lost people have reached out to DEEMI for help.

Volunteers are vital to search-and-rescue efforts. They work under the professional staff and are the boots on the ground that allow the wardens to cover vast areas. The volunteer groups are always well intentioned, but the larger the organization, the greater the variety of experience among volunteers. Sometimes they get pretty excited. They all want to find the lost person. Some of them want to feel a bit heroic, at least for the weekend—especially the volunteers who simply show up from the communities. Still, they can be useful in many ways. Fortunately, in each group of volunteers, there are usually leaders who can keep everyone on task without getting lost themselves. Because the Maine Association of Search and Rescue oversees the state's certifications and credentialing, Maine's volunteer organizations are organized and quite proficient. Decades ago, I sometimes felt that a rescue operation became more complicated when too many untrained volunteers showed up. There were one or two occasions when I worried more about some of the rescuers than I did about the lost person. Overall, the teams work well together, and one thing is always constant: everyone wants a good outcome. Maine has fourteen volunteer and professional search-and-rescue organizations, with several dog teams at their disposal.

The Maine wardens and volunteers are so good at finding people lost in the woods that it gets personal for them. Until the person is found, the wardens involved in the search hardly sleep. They have to remind each other to eat. Sometimes they aren't able to speak to their loved ones for days.

I've been to Gerry's final campsite several times. I've retraced the route I think she took after she left the AT. And my research assistant, Doug Comstock, and I agree: Gerry beat herself up on the first day and a half she was lost. The terrain is so difficult to negotiate, so dangerous, that we believe she climbed up the steep hill from the tiny brook on Wednesday afternoon, took a few steps at the summit, and, standing under the wispy branches of a hemlock tree, said to herself, *I am done!* There she would stay put. She would either be found there alive, with her tent set up on a bed of sticks, or not.

It is difficult to say how Gerry tried to reorient herself once she realized she was lost; while she didn't travel north or due west, it's possible that she just tried to hike it out, figuring she'd hit the AT or a road. It's also possible that she simply wandered, her travel dictated by the extremely difficult terrain. Gerry either had a plan to travel to ridgetops in an effort to find cell service or no plan at all.

The behavior of lost people is a challenging study.

CHAPTER SEVEN

What Is One to Do?

You were proud of your adventure,
We see your laugh on that picture,
Such a loss made me feel in torture.

—ABDERRAHMANE DAKIR

Getting lost seems to be a human thing. How we handle the situation differs widely. When my father was young and someone went missing, every able-bodied man around who was available scoured the woods for the lost soul. They were all "woodsmen" then, so the assumption was that the lost person was hurt and couldn't walk out on their own. Father used to speak of men occasionally becoming "woods queer"—a kind of psychosis from either living in the woods alone for too long or the stress of being lost—and actually eluding their rescuers, like the fellow in Wyoming who ran for days.

In an 1873 issue of the famous British scientific journal *Nature*, Charles Darwin contributed an article titled "Origin of Certain Instincts." In it, Darwin appears inclined to think that the instinctive recall of the sense of direction that animals seem to have (could be just their sense of smell) is shared by some people—if not mankind. He pointed out the uncanny sense of direction possessed by the Inuit in the far north, who maintained their bearings over the featureless Arctic terrain. The article prompted some interesting letters to the journal.

In the next issue of *Nature*, a chap named Henry Forde published a letter. It said:

In the wild parts of the state of West Virginia, even the most experienced hunters who frequent the woody mountains of this wild region are subject to a kind of shock, so that they suddenly lose their heads and feel that they are going in a direction directly contrary to that which they intended to follow. It is useless for their companions to reason with them and show them the position of the sun. Nothing can conquer this feeling, which is accompanied by a great nervousness and by a general sensation of distress and of uncertainty. The nervousness comes only after the seizure, and is not the cause of it.

Whatever anxieties Gerry Largay might have had before getting lost—fear of the dark, of being alone—they were surely compounded within minutes of her realization that she was lost. Still, every indication is that, no matter her lack of woodscraft, Gerry kept it together. She would hang tough.

Historically, other lost people have not always been as stoic as Gerry was. After losing her way on the AT, Gerry penned letters in her personal journal. Only a few of those entries have been made public, but one thing is clear: even under duress, she wrote eloquently.

Inchworm would try to light fires—though not effectively. On one day, she kept a fire going for a couple of hours. On another, desperation looming, she tried to light a dead spruce tree afire. Each time she worried about the fires getting out of control. She tried to signal aircraft as they flew in the distance. She tried to stay hydrated. But Gerry was fighting against a stark reality: After five days without food, the cognitive powers of human beings become altered significantly. After two weeks, they can become that of a toddler.

When I was in the search-and-rescue community in Wyoming in the 1980s, one of the directors was a surgeon and retired US Army colonel. He often suggested that too little was known of the psychology of lost people and that a better understanding might help in searches. He challenged me to undertake some unofficial research, for which I did not have the credentials. Long before the internet, the best I could do living four hundred miles from the nearest college was to write to several universities that offered correspondence schools—they would have the staff to handle mailed-in queries. With what little data I could find on lost-person behavior—some of it dating back to the early 1900s, including works by psychologist Alfred

Binet—I tried to come up with my own guide. All I knew about psychology at the time was that I probably would have hated Freud if I'd met him and that I might have loved Carl Rogers. I ended up drawing a triangle.

Many of us will remember from school the hierarchy of needs, a theory proposed in 1943 by psychologist Abraham Maslow in his paper "A Theory of Human Motivation," published in *Psychological Review*. Maslow subsequently extended his ideas of motivation to include his observations of humans' innate curiosity. He stressed the importance of focusing on the positive qualities in people—as opposed to treating them as a "bag of symptoms." Maslow stated that people are motivated to achieve certain needs and that some needs take precedence over others. He illustrated this theory with the schematic of a pyramid: Our most *basic need* for physical survival forms the base of the pyramid—food, water, warmth, rest—and this will be the first thing that motivates our behavior. Once the needs on that level have been fulfilled, the second-tier needs motivates us—safety and security—followed by third-tier psychological needs—love, friendship . . . belonging.

Using Maslow's diagram as a template, I drew a pyramidal map illustrating the best courses of behavior and action required for the lost person to give themselves the best possible chance for a favorable outcome. Each level of the pyramid detailed possible courses of action the lost person can take, and in what order, to help themselves. It was elementary. Much of it was common sense to anyone who grew up in the woods or on a farm, fishing and hunting. But that is only part of the population, so I tried to develop a comprehensive guide.

The *base* of the pyramid listed the most fundamental physiological needs: water source, food, warmth, and the best course of action in most cases—staying put.

The *second tier* up listed safety needs: improving shelter, protecting one's feet—do not panic, run around, and lose a shoe or sprain an ankle—and seeing to clothing—don't lose any clothing, and it might be necessary to alter some of the clothing; we lose up to 45 percent of our body heat through our heads, so put on a hat or make one.

I dedicated the *third tier* to behavioral needs: a lost person should focus hard on their wits, their state of mind—their behavior. This is of paramount importance. Work very hard to stay calm. Schedule parts of each day for resting, planning, gathering food if that skill is known to you, finding fuel for a fire, and so on. (Part of the plan should be to keep your shelter in sight while collecting.)

The *fourth tier* focuses on proactive needs: preparing signal fires, practicing compass work, observing, and preparing a plan for your self-extraction if you're not found by the fifth day.

The *top tier* of the pyramid simply says, "SAVED!!" whether from external rescue or self-rescue. (I was young and a slave to exclamation points in those days.)

I did not know what to call the diagram, so I shamelessly labeled it "Dee's Hierarchy of Needs for Lost People," which I realize is a sophomoric rip-off, but it wasn't meant for publication, or even to be a serious paper. It was a challenge from a leader of men whom I greatly admired. I included with the pyramid literature offering greater details, ideas, and a guide for each tier. The diagram is still in my journal from 1985, but my notes are long lost.

Fortunately, since then much work has been done by *actual* scholars in the field. One of my favorite papers was written in 1998 by Ken Hill. He has extensively researched how people remain spatially oriented as they move around in the environment and how they attempt to become reoriented when lost. He has conducted numerous studies related to land search-and-rescue operations, including lost-person behavior and decision-making processes of search coordinators. He has collected data on searches for lost persons in well over three hundred cases involving five hundred individuals. Dr. Hill has even studied the spatial behavior of serial offenders. His paper, "The Psychology of Lost," is an easy-to-read discussion of the concept of being lost. Hill is one of the most learned people on the topic of lost-person behavior, so it is telling when he says that "the truth is that little is known about the psychology of being lost." What we do have is behavior and patterns by lost people from the perspective of research.

Within a few hours of becoming lost, Gerry exhibited certain documented behaviors. She didn't stay put—not at first. We know that she was aware of the "stay put" adage, but she certainly didn't consider it immediately once she was lost, probably because she was so close to the trail. The AT, after all, had been her home for months. Surely she would pick up the trail in only a few moments. She never panicked. She never shed her clothing or her equipment. There's no evidence that she rushed what she was doing. But she was never spatially oriented, and she never formulated a reasonable plan. By her own reckoning, Gerry wandered for several miles. Eventually she worked hard to gain elevation, attempting to find cell service. When that didn't work, she decided it would be best to hunker down and stay put.

When lost, staying put works most of the time—especially if the person does so immediately once their predicament is realized. But people seldom do. Most walk, and they often walk with urgency. Some people run. In Maine, according to Warden Lieutenant Kevin Adam, nearly thirty people a year go missing while hiking the Appalachian Trail—which isn't a lot considering that's out of 350–520 annual calls for service throughout the state requiring search and rescue. Lieutenant Adam reports, "We have stats that say for all searches the person is located 92 percent of the time within twelve hours of us being notified and 97 percent of the time within twenty-four hours. Multiday searches are rare." Amazing, considering the difficulty of the terrain and how remote some parts of the state are.

Lieutenant Adam has been involved with the Maine Warden Service's Incident Management Team since 1995. "I started as a mapper/planner and did that for many years until I was first promoted to sergeant in 2008," says Adam, "then to lieutenant in 2009 when I took over responsibility for the search-and-rescue program. I am also the administrative team leader for the K-9 team because it has many connections to our search-and-rescue mission."

The Maine Warden Service is proud of its results, and should be, but the discipline of search and rescue is still evolving, more so in the past decade because of the reliance on technology in the backcountry. Add to that the fact that data collection and the study of lost-person behavior have only been seriously explored for fewer than forty years.

Quite often you will hear people say they "have a good sense of direction." For decades, scientists accepted that nearly all people possess a "sixth sense," a separate sensory mechanism for determining magnetic north. Dr. Hill points out, "While the specifics of this 'sixth sense' could not be described, it was considered to be very subtle and relatively undeveloped in most people, especially 'civilized' people living in cities where such a sense is rarely needed."

Where the special orienteering sense could be recognized most readily was in people from so-called "primitive" cultures, especially those in which way-finding skills are essential. Many people have marveled for centuries at the navigational skills of some South Pacific cultures, even to the point of suggesting the sailors in their canoes possessed a unique magnetic sense of direction. In fact, by 1700, tales of some of the islander's navigational skills had become legendary. In 1769, Lieutenant James Cook of the Royal Navy invited a "native navigator" by the name of Tupaia aboard his ship, *Endeavour*. Cook was astonished to find that Tupaia could draw his own map pinpointing all 130 islands within a 2,200-mile radius and was able to name seventy-four of them. He used—with the naked eye—celestial navigation, currents, birds, and the wind. But, Dr. Hill notes, "Such directional 'instincts' are the product of extensive training that typically begins in early childhood. Being the result of acquired expertise—rather than natural instinct—even the most experienced navigators of those societies are subject to error."

Mark Eddowes, an anthropologist who has lived in the Society Islands and has studied Polynesian culture for decades, agrees. "We reckon the process (of learning navigation) was deliberate and planned," said Dr. Eddowes in an interview by travel writer Rudy Maxa.

Each island group has a celestial star that fixes it within the map of the night sky. Centuries ago, you take young, crazy adolescents, put them in a canoe with the navigator. You can push them physically to the limit; it's an introduction to life for them—a passage into manhood. You find a new island and assign a star to it in the western sky.

The group would hang out on the island, eating fish, drinking from coconuts, and when a suitable time to return home came about, they could take the new knowledge with them. They collectively "have" the new star that already existed in the celestial map. Quite remarkable.

Growing up thrashing through the Maine woods with my friends, many times we were "turned around" or downright lost. But we always had a compass, and we always got out. It became a personal game to see how close to our vehicle we could come. Sometimes we would shove a stick into the ground to mark where we entered the woods. Typically, it would be fifty to a hundred yards from the stick, but as we got older, and better with a compass, we would occasionally step on the stick as we plunged out of the thick forest. Later in life, on some major expeditions, we negotiated the thickest jungles, most rugged mountains, and most forbidding deserts with only a compass.

Ken Hill maintains it is clear from his research that "having a 'good sense of direction' is based on the ability to take advantage of environmental cues, including feedback from one's own body movements, rather than a mysterious sixth sense." He speculates that in terms of being spatially oriented, or even knowing where we are, "Most people most of the time are much less oriented than they realize. Fortunately, this fact rarely becomes apparent to us, unless we make a wrong turn and have to regain our bearings."

Did Gerry have a good sense of direction? When interviewed by investigators in Maine, *Inchworm's* original Appalachian Trail hiking partner said no. Jane Lee told wardens that Gerry would often get turned around or after a rest break would begin walking in the wrong direction. Gerry's best friends, however, say she was very capable; she was good on trails and possessed great common sense. But after a couple of months on the trail, Jane Lee wasn't so sure. Under the stress of taxing her body and mind on such an arduous hike as the AT, Jane had noticed that a good deal of the time *Inchworm* was disoriented.

It is easy to speculate that Gerry, camped on that remote, desolate, forested ridge on the navy's SERE property, did not have a good sense of direction; in fact, there is plenty of evidence that suggests she didn't. But everyone who has hiked the Appalachian Trail has heard of somebody who started their hike in the morning taking a few steps in the wrong direction. Her *behavior* when lost, however, is of greater interest, because from that we may learn some things.

CHAPTER EIGHT

The Search

Let's go find her.

—DENNIS HAUG, US NAVY SENIOR CHIEF (RET.),
FORMER SERE SCHOOL SEARCH-AND-
RESCUE LEADER AND SURVIVAL EXPERT

Our greatest gift is good health, and it is often taken for granted. It is precarious, and the smallest obstacle can sweep it away—a virus, a fall, a bullet—leaving the strongest of us feeling vulnerable. Alone in the wilderness, it is more precarious still; help may be far away indeed. And in that moment, we often turn to faith—whether it is new to us or old—and if we don't have faith, there is only hope. But hope can be enough.

After close inspection of the route *Inchworm* took once she was lost, along with investigating her chosen campsite, one can conclude that, while she did keep a clear head while wandering, she wore herself out getting to her final site. She was most assuredly physically exhausted and a bit beaten up.

George, having slept in his car on the side of Route 27 near where the Appalachian Trail crosses the road, was troubled. But, being a manager, he kept his head and remained calm—at least outwardly. For two days, George continued to ask any northbound hikers who crossed the road whether they'd seen his wife: "Have you seen a woman, in her sixties, dark-rimmed glasses, green pack—possibly hiking alone, between Poplar Ridge and here?" No one had.

By early Wednesday afternoon, George had waited long enough. He called the state police. At 1:41 p.m., the Maine Warden Service was contacted.

Warden Lieutenant Kevin Adam was initially not overly alarmed. He knows the stats on hikers lost on the Appalachian Trail in Maine by heart. He felt that Gerry would be found or walk out in twenty-four hours. There's no reason why he wouldn't have felt that way.

When starting a search, the search manager—in this case, Lieutenant Adam—is the foundation. Their management skills affect every component of the search-and-rescue operation, including its outcome. "If the search manager loses control of the incident," says Ken Hill, "confusion reigns, tempers flare, the media gets hostile, and the search becomes a painful and protracted ordeal . . . ending in the necessity for recovery rather than a rescue."

Kevin Adam started putting the pieces of the puzzle together and gathering information. One warden called George while he waited at Route 27 on Wednesday within an hour of his call to state police. Another checked on him at 7:00 that evening. George explained the flip-flop hike. He told them what time Gerry had left Poplar Ridge two days earlier. She was a day late.

That evening, Lieutenant Adam assessed the situation and pored over maps. The first piece of the puzzle would be to confirm Gerry's direction of travel and determine her point last seen. Border-patrol agents and the state police put up signage along Route 4, letting hikers know a female hiker was missing. Warden Brock Clukey searched trails around Caribou Pond, north of the Appalachian Trail. Several volunteers from Mahoosuc Mountain Search and Rescue Team made their way to the Poplar Ridge Lean-To and worked their way north to Route 27 on Gerry's known route.

When a search is initiated for a missing person, an investigation is part of the process. Interviews had to be conducted. Adam delegated duties to other wardens, and local area search-and-rescue volunteers were called in to cover large swaths of forest where necessary. There was a lot to do. At first light on Thursday morning, the Appalachian Trail and area roads were searched on foot, by airplane and helicopter, with all-terrain vehicles, and in trucks. Gerry, now camped on the lonely ridge on navy land to the west of the AT, was not found.

Warden Investigators Philip Dugas and Joshua Bubier went to work obtaining an exigent—a type of search warrant used in law enforcement to legally obtain cell phone records. The warrant had to be carefully prepared and then signed off on by a judge in the Maine District Court in Farmington. On Thursday afternoon, the warrant was faxed to Cellco Partnership, Inc., a subsidiary of Verizon Wireless that processes exigents and procures cell phone data for law enforcement. In the application for the warrant, Warden Bubier was required to list his education and credentials and to make his case clear for the judge. He gave a brief synopsis of Gerry's known situation and ended with a telling paragraph: "Based on my education, training, and experience in search and rescue operations and based upon the above-mentioned facts and circumstances I believe that GERALDINE Largay is in a life and death situation. GERALDINE has been missing for over three days in what would be described as 'extremely difficult' terrain with limited resources such as food and water. Information contained within GERALDINE's cell phone records would assist investigators and searchers in located (locating) GERALDINE Largay."

The judge signed the warrant.

At the same time that the exigent warrant was being signed, based on reconstruction of events from site visits and known journal entries, Gerry became proactive. She established her route down the hill to the brook where she would go for drinking water. She knew now how easy it was to get lost; she wasn't going to chance it happening again and not be able to find her campsite. She would stay put until help arrived. She was a smart woman: she would've known to try to stay calm. It was a beautiful, sunny July day. She took her Mylar space blanket into the small open area sixty feet northwest of her tent site. Using some thread from her small sewing kit and some dental floss, she tied the corners to the branches of some young hackmatack trees, six feet off the ground. Obviously, she hoped reflections from the shiny surface would be seen by the search planes—if there were more.

That same morning, the search team was actively searching, investigating, or mobilizing. Thirteen game wardens, more than thirty-five volunteer rescue personnel, US Border Patrol agents, Maine State Police troopers, and local firefighters had converged on the temporary search headquarters that had been set up a Sugarloaf ski resort in the Carrabassett Valley, about seven and a half miles as the crow flies from where Gerry was camped. George, who was obviously stressed but still trying to stay collected, was questioned by several wardens and interviewed by Warden Pat Egan and again by Warden Investigator Phil Dugas. The state police were present. With every investigation of a missing person, immediate attention is given to the lost person's spouse or partner. The investigators initially deduced that all was well with Gerry and George and that they could move on to the hopeful search. Confidence was high that she would soon be found.

Wardens and searchers were assigned trailheads and questioned every hiker they encountered. There were many. Many of the old tote roads intersect or run parallel to the Appalachian Trail. These represent decision points for wandering, lost people. All established trails were divvied up and explored by either wardens or volunteers.

North Woods Law, an American reality television series, was underfoot as well. Originally set in Maine, the show followed numerous game wardens, and its camera crews were reasonably adept at staying out of the way of the officers as they performed their duties. Two of the wardens frequently profiled on the program, Scott Thrasher and Brock Clukey, were heavily involved with Gerry's search from the beginning.

Investigator Phil Dugas contacted hostels and lodges along the trail and asked the owners to contact people from their registries for possible information. Paul Renaud, co-owner of the Appalachian Trail Lodge in Millinocket, where Dottie Rust and Regina Clark had stayed before their hike south, called Dottie at her home in Maryland. "There's a hiker missing," he told her. "The Maine Warden Service has asked all hostel owners to call anyone who has stayed with them recently to see if they knew a hiker named *Inchworm*."

"I met her," said Dottie. "In fact, I took her picture at Poplar."

"You need to call the detective immediately," said Paul. He gave her Phil Dugas's phone number, and after a brief conversation, Dottie e-mailed him the photo of Gerry leaving Poplar Ridge. The men and women of the Warden Service put up posters using the photograph Dottie *.Com* Rust had taken Monday morning as *Inchworm* was leaving the Poplar Ridge shelter.

Dottie spoke with Lieutenant Adam and Investigator Dugas on the phone several more times, trying to recall everything she could about her time with Gerry. Both Dottie and Regina were very concerned. "I lost sleep worrying about her," said Regina.

By Thursday night, twenty-nine hours after George had first called the police to report Gerry missing, the game wardens had logged more than 111 man-hours either searching or investigating and 5.1 flight hours searching seventy nautical miles between Caribou Pond along the north side of the AT and the Sugarloaf Mountain area. Many more hours were worked by volunteers, the fire departments, and police.

That same evening, a fax arrived from Verizon. It was the exigent report. Finally, there was a real clue: At 2:36 Monday afternoon, a call had been placed to her phone. Gerry had not received the call, but it had created a ping—at the time, she had been just north of the Appalachian Trail, south of Caribou Pond, between Orbeton Stream and the Spaulding Mountain Lean-To.

By the evening of July 24, the tips started pouring in. There were so many calls that Adam had to authorize additional wardens to follow up on them. A few of the tips were helpful. Most were not. Some were even misleading. Once the search was under way, Adam had to deal intimately with the family members, and he faced the media daily. It all took singular focus.

Just after noon on Thursday, Investigator Dugas contacted the Redington naval facility and informed them of the missing hiker, Gerry's "point last seen," *and* her destination and hiking plans. The navy's SERE school employs some of the best searchers, man trackers, and rescue personnel on the East Coast—probably in the country. Being so close to the Appalachian Trail, SERE employees often help find lost people all over western Maine. Even though the SERE instructors are spread across New England when not on site, by Friday morning several navy search teams were in the area, ready to assist the Warden Service in the search for Gerry. They communicated with the wardens before starting each search, but the four- to six-man teams—one of them led by Senior Chief Dennis Haug—would search on their own, reporting back any sign or other information to Lieutenant Adam. Some of the men had driven all night to get to the search site by sunup. The navy men wanted Gerry found as badly as anyone.

The logistics Lieutenant Adam faces on a search in such formidable terrain are mind-boggling. His first objective was to learn the basics about Gerry and to establish her point last seen and her destination. He simultaneously had to consider the needs of those who were there to assist him—the wardens who were working with him, the police, the other hikers, and the civilian volunteers. He had to quickly evaluate the best way to employ them in the quest to find Gerry. He coordinated searches from the air and on the ground, and he strove to keep track of the dozens of volunteers.

The navy men were tuned in to their land. As commander of the SERE school Lieutenant Commander J. D. Walker said in 2016, "The Warden Service has a well-known competency. Their stats prove that. But in that isolated area along the navy property, we had personnel that knew every part of the place—every stone on the property because they've been over it hundreds of times. The bottom line is, our guys wanted to be there and were supportive of the effort. They put in a lot of man-hours."

On July 26, unbeknownst to them, the two four-man navy search teams were very close to Gerry—only one ridge away to the northeast of her position. The men were whistling and banging sticks on trees. There was no response.

A half hour's drive farther up Route 27 from where George was waiting for Gerry, the Stratton Motel is a popular hostel destination for Appalachian Trail thru-hikers. It's a simple, tastefully appointed motel only a few minutes' walk from the Stratton post office, and hikers have been washing trail dirt and sweat off in its showers for more than forty years. At 6:00 Thursday evening, Sue Critchlow, then manager at the Stratton Motel, called the police and was patched through to Warden Sergeant Terry Hughes. She told Hughes that a female hiker had called an employee at the motel. By the time it got to Lieutenant Adam, the message was that a hiker had heard about the missing woman and wanted someone to go to the trailhead to tell *Inchworm*'s husband that she had spent the night with Gerry at the Spaulding Mountain Lean-To the night before—Tuesday night. This tip *could* be the break the wardens had hoped for—a new point last seen—*if* it could be corroborated and investigated thoroughly. The transfer of information involved at least five people. Unfortunately, no one at the motel had recorded the calling hiker's real name or any contact information—only her trail name, *Kaleidoscope*. That meant it would be difficult to find the caller and, therefore, hard to corroborate. Still, it was information, and it had to be factored into the ongoing update of the time line. *Any* information is critical in the proper evaluation of the lost-person puzzle. Adam and his crew expanded the search area just in case.

By midday Friday, as Dennis Haug and the other navy searchers were combing the ridges near Gerry's campsite, a call came over the radio from the warden's command center. The team was working their way down the steep ridges on the SERE property toward Gerry's cell phone ping.

Navy contractor and corpsman Brett Pehowic, from Pennsylvania, was member of Haug's team. "We had so much confidence, experience, and knowledge of the area," said Pehowic. "If she was still near her ping, we were sure we were going to find her." To this day, he is upset about not finding her.

Acting on the previous day's tip from the Stratton Motel, the search-and-rescue coordinators let it be known that "searchers were needed nearer the Spaulding Shelter on the AT." The wardens assumed correctly that the navy men were capable of covering some ground in a hurry. Dennis Haug split his team, and several of the SERE school contractors beat their way east through the woods until they picked up the Appalachian Trail and headed north on the double toward the Spaulding Mountain Lean-To. They found no signs of Gerry.

Friday, July 26, was overcast, and rain showers were predicted. Six feet from Gerry's tent was an old birch tree. Well past maturity, its bark was peeling away on its own, shedding its skin to stem the growth of the bacteria underneath. Nine feet away was a little balsam, not six feet tall. Given that July was coming to a close, Gerry could have smelled the sweet, Christmas tree–like aroma that balsams give off that time of year—a smell that normally a person like her would notice and be pleased by, such a warm, familiar trace of nature. But the circumstances were not normal.

Now she was long overdue for her rendezvous with George, and whether he showed it in public or not, he was very anxious (a fact noted in several of the interviewing warden's notes). He stayed at the command center and tried to help, while at the same time his wife was committed to surviving as long as she could.

The human body is a complex thing, at once awesome and delicate, but it needs all its parts to work correctly. When Gerry worked and tried so hard to bushwhack and climb to find cell service or to punch her way out of her predicament, she taxed herself to the max. The day would come, all too soon, when she would no longer have enough food to sustain her.

That morning, just after sunup, the major search effort was in full swing. More wardens and volunteers were on the scene, including the navy search and survival experts. The area between the Poplar Ridge and Spaulding Mountain lean-tos was searched again. Hundreds of feet of forest on each side of the Appalachian Trail were combed, as were off-shoot trails north and west toward Sugarloaf Mountain and southeast toward the town of East Madrid. The Maine Forest Service and the state police were involved. The authorities followed every lead and conducted both a search *and* an investigation. When the rains didn't come as forecasted, a helicopter combed the area between Poplar Ridge and the Spaulding Mountain shelter for nearly ten hours. Gerry kept a log of her activities. According to one report, she heard the helicopter and frantically waved her red polar fleece jumper at the sound. The pilot couldn't see her through the thick forest canopy.

Warden Investigator Dugas kept questioning George and family members and hikers, trying desperately to find any piece of the puzzle he and Lieutenant Adam could put into place. George again had to answer personal questions: *Were they a happy couple? Was Gerry content? Was he content? Were there any financial troubles?* It had to have been hard on him.

Many of Gerry's friends were contacted throughout the United States. It was a painful time for everyone. For Lieutenant Adam and the rest of the game wardens, the initial evaluation of the scene was daunting: The area is vast, and in places the forest is impenetrable. In only a moment, Gerry's world had turned from the adventure of a lifetime to a living hell. How had this happened?

On the third day she was lost, she heard an airplane just to the southwest—a small one, flying low. She hurried to the small open area next to her tent site where the Mylar space blanket was tied and again tried to signal the aircraft. But the woods were too thick. She returned to her tent.

By the fourth and fifth days, Gerry was likely languishing, getting increasingly weaker, staring out of her tent at the drooping branches of the spruce and the balsams, waiting for help to arrive. She was forced by circumstance to confront her fear of being alone. High on that ridge in the blue-green slopes of the Redington range, she was *very* alone. We put our faith in dreams sometimes, and occasionally the dreams comfort us, but, for most of us, the one thing we cannot live without is love—in dreams or not. Love is precious and, if we are lucky, permanent. It is likely Gerry missed most the familiar comfort and reassurance of a loving touch. She wrote letters to her loved ones and suggested in at least one journal entry that she continued to pray, which suggests her love of family was strong and her faith remained. For many of us, a sense of community is the acme of living. When we cannot find it in our lives—even in cities and towns—we often look back and say things like "When we were kids, every mom in the neighborhood looked after all of us." The internet, and technology in general, is chipping away at the traditional sense of community, but not on the Appalachian Trail, where paradoxically people often go to find solitude only to find out that *community* is the thing. When Gerry stepped off the trail to relieve herself and got turned around, she lost that community. She lost any connection she had, except to God. Gerry had confided in fellow hikers that she strived to erase her fears through prayer.

Warden Dan Christianson, who was also involved from the first calls for help, searched trails and logging roads near Orbeton Stream where the Appalachian Trail crosses. For fourteen hours, he covered miles of woods and trails, both on foot and in his truck. Warden Josh Tibbetts put in thirteen hours. Warden Tim Place logged seventeen hours. The teams shared the awareness that time was critical. Lieutenant Adam, responsible for logistics and planning, hiked in to Spaulding Mountain Lean-To on the second day of the search to personally look for clues. There were none. If only Gerry had made a habit of writing in the shelter logbook. The wardens shook their heads; if someone's hiking alone, it only made sense to them.

On the afternoon on the fifth day, Lieutenant Adam met for the third time with some of the media. The wardens were becoming frustrated. There were thirty-eight game wardens involved, along with fourteen K-9s and scores of volunteers arriving on the mountains. In many places, the terrain was so difficult even the dogs had trouble walking. The game wardens alone logged more than four hundred man-hours. With no cell phone service in the area, Adam clung to optimism born of the Warden Service's track record. The thru-hikers were a helpful resource. "The Appalachian Trail has a pretty good communication system, actually," he told the cameras. "Everybody talks to one another, and everybody knows that she's missing . . . and no one has seen her."

By nightfall on Friday—Gerry had been lost for four days—the wardens were feeling a heightened sense of urgency. George had reported how much food Gerry had carried with her. She would be consuming no calories at all soon. According to those who knew her well, she had no known foraging skills. Some speculated that Gerry was hurt. The wardens knew too well that if she were not found soon, the odds of finding her alive were poor.

On Friday alone, the thirty-eight wardens involved with the search had racked up 416 man-hours. The K-9 teams had labored for fourteen hours. Four aircraft had been deployed, along with 112 volunteers. But there was no sign of *Inchworm*.

CHAPTER NINE

The Will to Live

It's not enough to be able to step along a trail. A body's got to have a little woodscraft.

—DONN FENDLER, OCTOBER 6, 2016,
AUTHOR OF *LOST ON A MOUNTAIN IN MAINE*

By Saturday, July 27, on her fifth day of being truly lost, Gerry was consuming less than one hundred calories per day. In another two days, there would be nothing. She knew people must be looking for her. Surely someone would find her. In her first few days off the trail, she had rationed her food and drunk the water in the two bottles she had packed with her. Though she had purchased a Sawyer-brand water-filtration system, she had not taken it with her on this leg of her hike. Having no water filter, the trepidation she felt about drinking straight from the little brook down the hill would have weighed heavily. Being a nurse, she knew all about *Giardia lamblia*, the microscopic parasite that can infect your small intestine. She also likely knew that the onset of giardiasis is about one to three weeks. Surely someone would find her before that.

Several contributing factors dictate the duration of survival without food: genetics, fitness, body weight, overall health before stopping caloric intake, the absence or presence of dehydration, and, importantly, the will to live. Humans *can* survive without food, if properly hydrated, for more than sixty days. Most starving people last thirty to forty days. Some die much earlier. The most common cause of death in extreme cases of starvation is a myocardial infarction (heart attack) or organ failure. Some studies suggest both occur most often when the body mass index reaches approximately 12.5. For a woman of Gerry's height—five feet, five inches—that would mean *seventy-five* pounds. Some researchers maintain that body composition is important; individuals with a greater percentage of body fat have a greater reserve of stored calories to burn. Research suggests that females might have a slight advantage over males because they require less caloric intake. But the one factor no researchers investigate when studying starvation is desire—the individual's sheer will to live.

History, distant and near, is riddled with tales of human starvation—both voluntary and involuntary (Mohandas Gandhi reportedly performed a total of fourteen hunger strikes). Some of the most evocative stories occurred at the poles, especially in the Arctic, where hundreds of men became stranded while seeking first gold and then the elusive and theoretical Northwest Passage to the East Indies.

In the spring of 1845, Sir John Franklin of the Royal Navy set out with two ships, HMS *Erebus* and HMS *Terror*, for the Canadian Arctic. Provisioned for three years, the expedition planned to poke around the Arctic islands and ice floes and, heading east to west, find a waterway through to present-day Alaska. The expedition members, with twenty-four officers and 104 other ranks, were never seen alive again. Well, not by white men, at least.

Throughout the first year and a half of the expedition, the Inuit (previously called "Eskimo" by outsiders, or, in Franklin's day, "Eskimeaux") had tried on several occasions to communicate with the expedition, to trade and exchange knowledge. The officers ignored them, considering them savages who would be an annoyance rather than a valuable resource. The Inuit, standing comfortably on the ice in their ventilated sealskin and polar bear–fur coats, pants, and boots—well fed because of ten thousand years of experience surviving in the Arctic—watched the officers stroll away from them on deck, stomping their feet while they froze in their Cotswold-wool coats and felt boots. A little over a year later, seeing the Englishmen dragging their lifeboats across the frozen ground, desperately trying to make their way to a Hudson's Bay Company outpost a thousand miles to the south, the Inuit kept their distance, understanding that they weren't wanted. If a relationship had been fostered earlier, the outcome of Franklin's expedition might have been very different. Perhaps

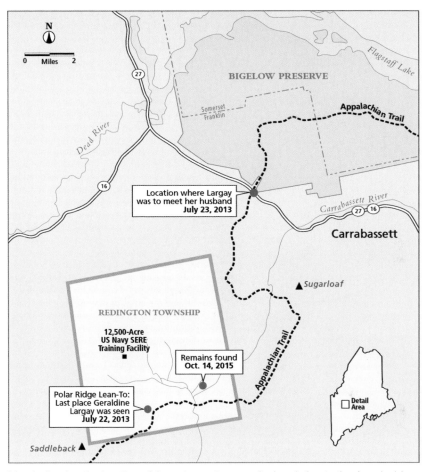

Map indicating the location of Gerry Largay's campsite in relation to the Appalachian Trail and the US Navy SERE (Survival, Evasion, Resistance, and Escape) property.

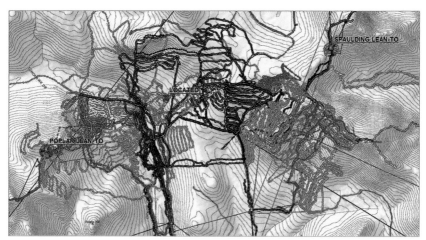

Mapping the search for Gerry. The red lines indicate K-9 search routes.

Gerry helping her friend Betty Anne Schenk with research in the South Pacific.
BETTY ANNE SCHENK

Gerry loved the birds of the South Pacific.
BETTY ANNE SCHENK

Mount Greylock surprise: Gerry and Jane Lee on the AT in June 2013, having their picture taken by Kit Parks.

KIT PARKS

The last photo of Gerry, taken as she was preparing to leave Poplar Ridge Lean-To.
DOTTIE RUST

Bill Green and Dennis Haug at Gerry's final campsite.

D. DAUPHINEE

This memorial for Gerry was created at the location of her final campsite.

D. DAUPHINEE

Dennis takes a private moment at the memorial built for Gerry at her campsite.

D. DAUPHINEE

Gerry's friend Dottie Rust pays her respects at Gerry's memorial.
D. DAUPHINEE

Dottie leaves a memento at Gerry's memorial.

Dottie is comforted by her husband.
D. DAUPHINEE

A memorial gathering to honor Gerry.

KIT PARKS

The old Railroad Road lies about 1,800 yards from Gerry's campsite.

DOUG COMSTOCK

The border of the US Navy SERE training facility. Note the animal bones hung as a warning.

D. DAUPHINEE

Doug Comstock and Dennis Haug repair Gerry's memorial site after the windstorm of 2017.

D. DAUPHINEE

the Inuit could have taught the Brits how to survive in the Arctic wilderness. The Inuit would do just that on many subsequent expeditions, several of which were rescue missions and, later, recovery voyages searching for the Franklin ships and men. Survival skills might have made all the difference to the British expedition.

For decades no one knew exactly what their fate had been, and search efforts in the Arctic were massive. Nine years after the *Erebus* and the *Terror* had left England, Scottish surgeon, surveyor, and explorer John Rae was surveying the Boothia Peninsula for the Hudson's Bay Company, some distance south of where Franklin's ships had sunk. Rae was a man keen to learn from the Inuit, and he respected them. It was from a band of hunters that Rae learned the fate of the Franklin expedition: the ships had become stuck and the sailors had tried to reach safety on foot, eventually dying of starvation and the cold. The Inuit told Rae that, in the end, the men had resorted to cannibalism. Rae made his report to the Admiralty, but it infuriated the authorities and Lady Jane Franklin, Sir John's dutiful wife, who was herself a force to be reckoned with. They all tried to discredit the Scotsman. Even Charles Dickens (a rock star in his day) publicly accused Rae of being "absurdly wrong"; no British naval man, Sir Franklin's defenders insisted, would ever sink to that level. And yet they did.

The Inuit hunters reported that there had been plenty of seals and polar bears in the area where they saw the starving men. Because of the disdain the Englishmen had so clearly displayed in the past, the hunters had feared approaching the sailors and so had moved on (though one Inuit story has two hunters passing close enough to interact with the dying Englishmen, giving them what little food they could spare without endangering their own lives). Eventually, the remains of the last men were found on the desolate King William Island, far to the south of the ships' last-known whereabouts; the Inuit—and Dr. John Rae—had been correct all along. But the clues during the search had been few and, even once found, had been largely disbelieved.

In 1982, University of Alberta professor of anthropology Owen Beattie flew to King William Island with a small team of researchers to retrace the steps of the last of the survivors who had dragged their boats southward along the ice. They found the skeletal remains of several of the men. When they studied the bones in their lab, they found unusually high traces of lead in them—presumably from the relatively new (in 1845) technique of soldering together the tin cans for storing the expedition's preserved meats and vegetables. Heavy amounts of lead had been in contact with the food for months and years.

Two years later, Beattie and a larger team returned to the Arctic, this time to exhume the graves of three of Franklin's men, buried farther north on Beechey Island. The frozen remains were ghastly, and remarkably well preserved. The researchers stripped the dead of their cotton and wool clothing and marveled at the telltale Y-shaped incisions from autopsies that had been performed aboard ship, 138 years earlier. Tissue samples were taken, which later showed high levels of lead, and the men were photographed and returned to their resting places.

There are people who believe the Franklin expeditioners were killed not by lead poisoning from meat tins—which might have led to poor decision making and a sickened, deconditioned state—but rather by poor survival skills born of prejudices that prevented their gaining knowledge from indigenous people. Instead of learning from the Inuit how to hunt and survive in the Arctic, as European men after them would do, Franklin's officers chose to rely on English fortitude and sheer will to succeed, and if they perished along the way, they thought, then the day would not be lost: they would have their glory.

Thirty-five years after Sir John Franklin died aboard his ship, a US Army officer and Civil War veteran from Massachusetts, Adolphus Washington Greely, sailed up Davis Strait along the west coast of Greenland—the same waters Franklin had sailed—and into the Arctic. Greely's polar expedition had been commissioned by the US government to collect astronomical and polar magnetic data and to look for clues of yet *another* lost Arctic exploration that had set out a few years earlier. The Greely crew erected a small compound of huts on the west coast of Ellesmere Island. The plan was for the expedition to receive annual resupplies at the site, but because the Davis Strait stayed covered in pack ice for twenty-four months, two consecutive supply parties failed to reach Greely and his men. The party left their compound in August 1883 and walked south.

Their story of survival is epic; for nine months, the men endured an Arctic winter in canvas tents—for the last two months with no food. After months of rationing, Greely wrote in his journal, "Chewed up the foot of a fox this evening raw. It was altogether bone and gristle." When at last they were rescued in June 1884, the entire party was near death. Greely had had one man shot for pilfering the scant rations of food stores. One of the rescued men later died aboard ship on the way home, and in New York, the anticipation of welcoming the heroes of the Greely expedition was tempered by tales that had leaked about possible cannibalism back on Ellesmere. Again, the survival skills were woefully lacking within the expedition. Knowledge of hunting and surviving in the Arctic wilds had been inadequate. Stories abound of men in the Arctic, in the throes of desperation, past all earthy succor, eating their shoe leather. Scores of starving men would lie down on the frozen ground under starry skies and die. It wouldn't be until the early 1900s that survival skills—beyond firing a gun—would finally be considered critical. The importance of basic survival skills is still evolving, perhaps more important in today's world because of society's increasing reliance on technology.

The most famous survival story in Maine took place in July 1939, when twelve-year-old Donn Fendler was separated from his family on a foggy, rainy day near the summit of Mount Katahdin. His disappearance launched a massive manhunt that became front-page news throughout the nation. Game wardens, hundreds of volunteers, and two bloodhounds known for their man-tracking capabilities joined the effort to locate the boy. No searchers found him. The dogs never picked up a scent. Yet Donn survived for nine days without food or proper clothing before first following the downward flow of a stream, then a telegraph wire, and then a different stream that led out of the woods near Stacyville, Maine. Subsisting on only a few berries he'd found along the way and drinking water as he came across it, the boy had hiked an astonishing ten to fourteen miles a day, in the same kind of difficult terrain that Gerry would encounter seventy-four years later. Donn's trek was made more remarkable because on the second day he lost his sneakers. The next day he lost his pants. He wandered at least fifty miles through the woods and waded brooks barefoot and pantless. Because of all his meandering in trying to find his way out of the wilderness, he covered at least eighty-six miles to advance a mere thirty-eight. Gerry—if her reckoning is accurate—covered "3–4 miles" on her first day of being lost but advanced only about seven-tenths of a mile.

Donn Fendler was a boy of great faith and a Boy Scout. When he first became separated from his hiking party on the cloud-covered summit of Mount Katahdin, he realized he ought to stay put but knew he couldn't. Dressed in a light jacket and dungarees, he knew he wouldn't be able to spend the night near the cold, exposed peak. He was compelled to move. He also knew from his father and his scouting knowledge that he should find a brook, even a trickle, and follow it downstream. He did, but unfortunately, without a compass, he wandered down the "back" side of the mountain—toward the west . . . the wrong side. His efforts to find some help in that direction would be multiplied many times over.

On the ninth day of his wandering, Donn dragged himself onto the East Branch Penobscot River, fourteen miles above the town of Grindstone, quite close to the village of Stacyville. Across the river were some sporting camps. Hoarse, gaunt, nearly faint from exposure and lack of food, and bleeding from cuts, scrapes, and bug bites, Donn got the attention of the camp owners. They were astonished to see the boy. By canoe, they collected Donn and placed him in the main camp. They called the authorities. A doctor called the camp with instructions on how to care for him until help could arrive. Again, Donn was national news. As an adult, decades after the sporting-camp owners had rescued him, Donn produced a book with writer and illustrator Joseph Burke Egan. It has become a staple in many Maine schools, and Donn traveled throughout the state each year to tell his tale to the children. Donn's father had recommended he and Egan write the story to show children what was possible with "faith and determination."

In the autumn of 2016, I wrote Donn a letter, addressed to his summer home in Newport, Maine, asking whether we could get together and discuss Gerry Largay's ordeal and his own. Like all Mainers, Donn was familiar with her disappearance, and he called me with an invitation to his home. On October 6, a Thursday, I showed up exactly on time. (Donn, at age ninety, was a retired army colonel. I figured I'd better be punctual.) We sat on the porch of his place on Sebasticook Lake, drank iced tea, and talked about Gerry. I told him about my experiences with lost-person behavior, and he looked at me wistfully, with steely blue eyes. Woven into the conversation were memories of his own ordeal in the woods seventy-seven years earlier. He seemed to remember much of it as it were yesterday.

"Have you read my book?" he asked me.

"Yes," I said. "You came to Vine Street School in Bangor when I was nine. You signed a book for me."

Donn smiled. "I've been to a *lot* of schools."

We talked about the condition of his feet while he'd been lost, and about the state of his mind. "The stress is enormous," he said. "The stress can not only fatigue you, but it can affect your decision making." Donn thought for a moment, and before I could prompt him for more, he said, "Add to the stress the physicality aspects: swollen feet, cut feet, sore joints from hunger and the cold . . . it takes a toll. You know, I had hallucinations, and I don't mean once I started to starve, but right away. I had them on the second day. To this day I don't know if they were dreams or not."

I said, "I remember from the book that you fainted a couple of times."

"More than a couple," Donn said. "On the eighth and ninth day, I was walking, but for some of the time I believe I was 'out on my feet.'"

By the time Donn was finally rescued, he had lost sixteen pounds, weighing only fifty-eight. He was emaciated and worn to a frazzle from stress and the relentless mosquitos.

"I never went into the woods again—even for a moment—without a compass and at least a good idea of where I was and which way I'd have to go to get out," Donn remarked. "I also learned how to make a fire several different ways. Thank God I never had to rely on that."

Donn said if there was to be a legacy, he "wanted to be a help to future generations." As if an afterthought, he said, "Maybe my book will do that."

It made me think about Gerry's legacy, if she was to have one beyond her family and friends.

When pressed about Gerry, Donn emphasized that everybody who attempts to thru-hike the Appalachian Trail should be prepared beyond trail knowledge—beyond knowing about layering clothes, filtering water, mail drops, and packing light. They should learn what to do if they get lost. In Donn's words, "It's not enough to be able to step along a trail . . . they should have a little woodscraft."

"Three things helped me get through my ordeal," he said. "My faith—I still believe in guardian angels—my experience with the Boy Scouts, and the will to live." Donn paused. "We all are born with the will to live. Rarely people lose it. Nobody wants to die . . . you fight. You just fight for all you're worth."

When I left the interview, I told him that I might have some more questions once I had digested the information. We agreed to talk again on the phone the following Tuesday, but we couldn't.

Four days later, in the wee hours of Monday morning, Donn died.

CHAPTER TEN

All Leads Explored

The purpose of life is to live it, to taste experience to the utmost, to reach out eagerly and without fear for newer and richer experience.
—ELEANOR ROOSEVELT

At certain times, all spoken language is inadequate. This becomes clear when one tries to explain to a family that a loved one is lost and there is no knowledge of their fate. Lieutenant Adam, several of the wardens, and the Maine State Police tried to keep George Largay and the rest of Gerry's family members abreast of the search efforts. There was pain on all sides.

By Saturday, July 27, the fifth full day Gerry was lost, the major search effort was at its zenith. Helicopters searched both sides of the Appalachian Trail again. Planes were used. And again Gerry heard the planes. Several dog teams split up and combed the woods. Horses and ATVs roamed the tote roads. More than one hundred men and women volunteers bushwhacked through the forests. Dozens of local people searched on their own, feeling they knew the area better than anyone—people from the villages of East Madrid, Barnjum, and Phillips. Maine Forest Service and US Border Patrol personnel assisted the wardens in any way they could. Gerry wasn't found.

Kit Parks—a woman Gerry had met at Warren Doyle's Appalachian Trail Institute—had sensed something about *Inchworm* and enjoyed her enthusiasm; they had quickly become friends. Now she showed up with Jane Lee to join the search. They spoke with wardens and the Largay family. The two intrepid women hiked from Route 27 in Stratton (where George had waited for Gerry to show) to the Spaulding Mountain

Lean-To. They spent the next four days looking for her, hoping to be reunited with *Inchworm* on a trail somewhere.

It was also on Saturday that Gerry's food supply was essentially gone. She spent some time improving her tent site, but she likely spent a good deal of time in her sleeping bag. She read what precious little reading material she had—including an excerpt from Terry *Blue Moon* Bliss's trail blog, which she'd printed out after meeting and hiking with him in late June and early July. She added more pine needles, twigs, and sticks under her tent to build up a sort of platform to try and keep the floor of her tent dry. The woods were very damp from the torrential rainfall three days earlier and from the record rainfall throughout the previous month. In the forest, night is a time for animals and for those people open to the sounds in the dark. Though Gerry feared being alone at night, she was dealing with it the best she could. She carried a rosary . . . perhaps it helped assuage her fears. Without a doubt, people who are lost experience a high emotional arousal, and typically—like Donn Fendler seventy-four years before—they become distraught during the ordeal. The stress can even cause nausea and abdominal pain, which are probably from what is called a *vagal response*.

The vagus nerve is the tenth of twelve pairs of cranial nerves and is the longest in the body. It emanates from the brain and passes through the neck, very close to the jugular vein, from where it wanders through, behind, and around various organs in the neck, chest, and abdomen. The word *vagus* means "wanderer" in Latin and is a perfectly suited name. The vagus nerve intervenes with many functions, from breathing to heartbeat to bowel movements. It also controls the parasympathetic system, which transmits signals of nervousness or calm, anger or relaxation. It is safe to say Gerry's sympathetic nervous system was activated.

As Dr. Ken Hill notes, all emotional experience is part mental or cognitive and part physiological. Physiologically, intense stress can involve certain glandular secretions (such as sweaty palms or a rush of adrenalin) as well as stimulation of a part of the brain called the *limbic system*. It is in the limbic system that physiological and cognitive reactions appear to interact. "When arousal is intense (such as in life and death situations), thoughts tend to scatter in irrelevant directions, making the person unable to concentrate on solving even simple problems," reports Dr. Hill. "Also, too much arousal can reduce the number of environmental cues the person can perceive, thus interfering with the recognition of familiar objects, people, or places."

Certainly, Gerry felt a wide range of emotions. Judging by the few journal entries made public, her writing in the note left for her discoverer, and by what has been related to me, I believe that on an emotional level Gerry coped with her situation better than many would have. She would have relished the time sleeping—when it came. In sleep, it would be easy to forget the shadows in the trees in the waning light of evening. When sleep didn't come, and she could not ignore the shadows, her faith would have to carry the weight of her fears.

Though she built no hearth for a fire—for warmth or as a signal for search parties—Gerry looked around and found a couple of small, dead spruce trees about eighty feet to the north of her tent. She tried to start a signal fire by lighting some twigs and leaves at the base of them. One little fire burned up the trunk of the tiny tree about three feet before it went out. The other got going, but she put it out before it got too big. Unfortunately, it would appear that Gerry didn't know about the bark of northern white birch trees. Eight feet from the flap of her tent was a white birch tree, one well past maturity. The old bark was peeling away. The birch bark annually peels back on its own, making room for new bark growth. On old, dying trees the new bark doesn't come, making the tree vulnerable to bacteria and deterioration. The bark of birch trees contains a natural oil (betulum, or betula alba) that burns extremely well and will light even when wet. The bark of that birch tree could have helped her, had she known. If she had gathered enough of it, she could have started a fire even in the pouring rain. There was fire-starting help all around her: Just outside her tent were several balsam trees. The resin from the balsam trunks is quite flammable and makes an excellent fire-starting aid. Smear the resin onto tinder and some kindling, and you're guaranteed the fire will light. If she had known to snap a large pile of balsam branches to dry out, they could quickly be thrown on a small, smoldering hearth that could have been kept going all day, causing great, billowing clouds of smoke. As it was, her fires were unsuccessful. She kept them too small and contained; it is apparent that she was worried the flames might get out of control. When I spoke with a retired Maine game warden in 2016 about her fire attempts, he said, "I would've had Smoke Jumpers raining down on me to put out the forest fire." Of course, he was exaggerating, but I understood his point.

Knowing Gerry's point last seen (Poplar Ridge) and the location of her cell phone ping, the navy SERE instructors hit the search hard. The wardens didn't have to worry about the navy men, as they might some of the noncertified volunteers wanting to help. They could be left to their own devices and could live in the woods for weeks if they needed to. At the end of the day, when the wardens called to tell them to "come out of the woods," the navy contractors wouldn't call it quits. They had been buoyed earlier when they had had found a Vibram soled footprint in the mud. It was in an area where there ought not to have been a booted track. The two teams had a meeting. Senior Chief Haug told the teams, "If this were your mother, you'd want her to know that someone was looking for her." Of course they all felt the same. The men searched until after dark and went out again on Saturday morning before daylight. Much of the land the navy men searched was *their* land, and it is some of the toughest terrain in the search area. They knew it better than anyone. They were determined.

The monumental task of planning and then executing such a large search can take a toll on the operational leader. Lieutenant Kevin Adam and his wardens kept running what information they had through their minds: *last known location . . . last cell phone ping . . . Gerry's direction of travel . . . the terrain.* The wardens were obliged to follow every lead. Several of the personnel from the Maine Warden Service and the state police were busy taking phone calls and reading e-mails with the flood of tips and offers to help. Some people even called from out of state simply with advice for the searchers; having looked over maps and hearing the news reports, they felt sure they knew where she was.

Adam reached out to the public for any help. He briefed and got input from the Maine Appalachian Trail Club, but, unfortunately, no one at the MATC—or the warden service—thought to ask the opinion of Dr. David Field, the man who had built the section of trail where Gerry was missing *and* had acquired the corridor of land on either side of the section. Moreover, he had maintained the section of trail for fifty-seven years. Yet he wasn't consulted. But, as one of the wardens later sadly pointed out, "We can't know who *everybody* is"—which, of course, is true.

Meanwhile, David Field was sitting at home, waiting to be called. He understood very well how stretched the searchers were and didn't want to be one more person for them to deal with if they didn't need his help.

The message Gerry had sent George when she first became lost is haunting: *Can u call AMC to c if a trail maintainer can help me. Somewhere north of woods road. Xox.* Though David had recently handed upkeep of his section of the trail over to younger maintainers, he was still fit and capable. He would have been one of the people to call for advice. Lieutenant Adam recalls having met up several times with the Maine Appalachian Trail Club and the ATC for input, but "[David's] name never came up. We would have liked to talk with him."

In that first week since Gerry had gone missing, the search efforts had grown into one of the largest searches in the history of the state. As the major news outlets continued to run Gerry's story, Adam was required to find the time to meet with the media. Five days into the search, he faced the cameras. "It is a mystifying search," he told reporters, "because we've done a lot of tactics that would normally produce results by now. Most times, hikers get lost at decision points—trail crossings, road crossings, a fork in the trail—and there were quite a few decision points for her but no evidence which way she went."

Some one thousand miles to the south, in Tennessee, Warren Doyle started getting calls at the Appalachian Trail Institute. Like him or not, Doyle probably has hiked the AT more than anyone alive, and he does have a following. People thought he ought to know that Gerry had gone missing. Doyle called the wardens on Saturday. He offered some thoughts about the likely spots where she could get into trouble. The assumption by many had been that she had gotten off the AT and injured herself. The warden investigators told Doyle they had already "searched all the obvious places" but wanted to know more about his Appalachian Trail Institute. The conversation quickly turned from Doyle's offers of assistance to an inquiry into his teachings.

Most Maine game wardens have grown up in the state of Maine and were taught woodcraft and compass work from a young age. They asked Doyle questions about his program: Did you teach her how to use a compass? Did you go over fire starting? How about what to do if lost off the trail?

Doyle replied, "No, no, and no. It's not that kind of a school. I don't teach from a curriculum. And I don't teach survival skills. If a student were to ask me, I'd tell them commonsense things like going downhill and downstream." Doyle was feeling a little pressed by the wardens and frustrated. The game wardens, who consider themselves true woodsmen, couldn't wrap their heads around the fact that people taking an Appalachian Trail course might not receive basic instruction in woodsmanship. Doyle tried to explain that the course was meant to address the many difficulties thru-hikers would likely encounter *on* the AT. The only aspects they covered *off* the trail were overnights, hostels and motels, mail drops, road crossings, and other routine aspects of the thru-hike. The course was more geared toward preparing hikers for the mental rigors of the Appalachian Trail.

The wardens simply wanted to know how prepared Gerry was for her situation. They were still trying to determine what they were dealing with: What skills did Gerry have that might help her with her survival? Sifting through the dozens of tips pouring in, they were reaching for anything that might help them direct their search in such formidable terrain. All they got from Doyle was the truth: Gerry was a well-equipped, capable hiker who was mentally well prepared. He knew that she had meticulously planned her AT hike, and he had never conversed with her about backcountry-survival skills. Some of the wardens were frustrated that Gerry might not have the knowledge to aid in her self-rescue.

As the searchers worked, Gerry's family reached out to the media for any help. Perhaps there was a hiker out there who had finished the trek and hadn't heard of *Inchworm*'s plight . . . or had spent time with Gerry between the Poplar Ridge and Spaulding Mountain shelters and might have the clue that would narrow the search. Only when bonds are tested do we realize their strength: Gerry's family and their closest friends pulled together. George, for his part, kept a stoic face for the media. He saw no use in weeping for the cameras.

Throughout the weekend of July 27 and 28, the wardens, members of the Maine Association for Search and Rescue, US Border Patrol, Maine State Police, Maine Search and Rescue Dogs, and citizen volunteers blanketed the area. Navy SERE personnel focused on the corridor of land between the Appalachian Trail and their property, sweeping again down steep ravines toward Gerry's known cell phone ping. Many of the searchers acted on the cryptic tip from the Stratton Motel suggesting that someone had spent the night with her at Spaulding Mountain Lean-To.

On Saturday, an eighteen-year-old southbound hiker from Tennessee, Trevor *Crunchmaster* Pyke, was taking a zero day in Rumford while section hiking southbound with two of his cousins, Josh Smith and Matt Johnson. While the three were resting, eating pizza, and watching a Red Sox game, the police called Trevor's cell. They told him about Gerry. They talked for about fifteen minutes and asked if the boys would be willing to backtrack on their trip to be interviewed.

"They believe *Milkrun* [Josh], Matt, and I were possibly the last ones to see her," Trevor wrote on his Facebook page. "So tomorrow, the game wardens have asked us to go to the command post so that we can possibly help with locating her. We don't know much information but hopefully we will remember where we could have seen her."

The three teenagers did show up to help. Unfortunately, based on Gerry's description and what images they had of her at the time, the boys were unable to positively identify her. Trevor had frequently hiked faster than his cousins, reporting to wardens that he had descended southbound on the AT from Lone Mountain between 3:00 and 3:30 p.m.—farther west of where Gerry had left the trail. He came upon a female hiker, he told them. "She appeared to be played out," he told the warden. "I didn't really get a good look at her." She was wearing distinctive glasses, he said. There wasn't much to go on. The cousins did see a woman sitting near the trail on their way south but could not be sure it was *Inchworm*.

Lieutenant Adam also reached out to the mainstream media and social media. "I'm promedia," Adam explained. "The media can be extremely helpful in the early days of a search. Later on, if the search doesn't go well, the media will still want to report on it, and if there isn't any real news, they sometimes seek conflict to make things interesting. Not all of them will do that, but it happens."

Using the shelter logs collected at Poplar Ridge and Spaulding Mountain, the wardens posted requests for information on Appalachian Trail websites. On the same day the police called Trevor Pyke, the Maine Warden Service posted to the popular AT forum at WhiteBlaze.net:

UPDATE: SEARCH FOR GERALDINE LARGAY—July 27, 2013: Maine Game Wardens are seeking information concerning missing AT hiker Geraldine Largay who uses the trail name "inchworm" from the following hikers using the trail names: "Cowboy", "Marathon", "Postman", "Breeze", "Paranoid", "Crunchmaster", "Harpo/Groucho", "Ice Pack/SOBO '13", "Luke 11:9", "Sandman", "BBTGR", and ".com/Queen".

Warden investigators need to speak with the listed hikers to determine and verify if Geraldine was seen between the Poplar Ridge Lean-To and the Spaulding Mountain Lean-To on the Appalachian Trail. Warden investigators also need to verify if Geraldine stayed overnight at the Spaulding Mtn. Lean-To Monday night July 22 into Tuesday morning July 23. The Warden Service also wants to inform bear baiters baiting in the search area to be on the lookout for Mrs. Largay.

Those with any information should call the Public Safety Communications Center in Augusta . . .

Lieutenant Adam worked to effectively deploy the scores of volunteers—especially the nonprofessionals who simply show up or try to search in the same areas independently. Unfortunately, with spotty or absent cell service in the area, communication with the command center became difficult. For example, the navy survival experts searching the woods had clear communication with the SERE school through its landline, by which they could convey messages to Lieutenant Adam's command.

In the first few days of an extended search, it's important for the search leaders to try to keep a record of which areas have been "cleared" by the professional searchers, especially by the K-9 teams. If an area is searched hard by locals who want desperately to help before the K-9s have been deployed, the area can be "contaminated" with many scents, giving false scent alerts to the dogs.

On Monday, July 29, Todd Remaley (chief ranger of the Appalachian National Scenic Trail) and Travis Baker (ranger at Monocacy National Battlefield in Maryland) happened to be in Maine. They arrived at the command post to offer assistance. Though they were acquainted with the Appalachian Trail, it was unlikely that Lieutenant Adam would send the men off the trail into the dense terrain unfamiliar to them, but they could help facilitate communications with the Maine Appalachian Trail Club. MATC might have some members unknown to the wardens who could be helpful. Perhaps they could be used as liaisons between the wardens and the AT hikers and trail maintainers. The number of people a manager can effectively supervise and control is limited, especially during a massive search-and-rescue operation. Lieutenant Adam had to constantly delegate authority to assistants—other wardens, for whom the manageable span of control also applies. Several times a day, Adam would confer with his team—especially at night—to draw upon all available expertise to assign priorities to different segments to the search locale.

The most important fact during a search-and-rescue operation is the PLS—place last seen, or, in some SAR communities, point last seen—by a witness. The PLS forms the basis of the search planning. Gerry's PLS had been established when Dottie .Com Rust had snapped her photo just as Inchworm was leaving Poplar Ridge Lean-To the previous Monday morning. Or was it when a hiker thought she saw Gerry at Spaulding Mountain Lean-To on Tuesday night? In the end, the only confirmed PLS was from Dottie and her hiking partner, Regina Clark.

Typically, once notified of the PLS, the operation leader—in this case, Lieutenant Adam—will make a quick assessment of the situation and send out teams for "hasty searches"—or Type I searches, as they are known in some SAR communities. These hasty-search teams are normally the first ground searchers into the field. They search from the lost person's PLS and along the direction of travel, if known. Hasty teams search trails, drainages, water boundaries, and other areas where the lost person is most likely to be found in order to locate the subject as quickly as possible. Hasty searches aren't meant to be large, thorough searches. Along the Appalachian Trail in Maine, most of the time lost people are found during the hasty searches.

The hasty searches are followed by K-9 searches and by "grid" searches—or Type II searches—with professionals and volunteers spaced more than fifty feet apart. The searchers move in a parallel fashion for a designated distance, then step sideways and travel back in the direction from where they started. The Type II grid searches can be very effective and are often used in heavy vegetation when it is expected that the subject will be responsive. Though I know of people found in such ways, in my years in SAR we never found someone in a formal grid search—only when traveling in small, four- to eight-man teams, such as the ones the wardens and the navy SERE instructors were conducting.

As a last resort, a closed-grid "sweep"—or Type III search—is used. This technique involves very narrow spacing between searchers who are sometimes almost shoulder-to-shoulder. Type III searching is quite slow and inefficient but is often employed when it is suspected the subject may be unresponsive, such as with a person with dementia or with small children, who have been known to hide from rescuers.

Lieutenant Adam's considerations were vast. He took Gerry's personal profile, provided by George, and made check lists of resources as they arrived on the scene. He then weighed them with maps of the area and with Gerry's PLS. He combined them with schedules, plans, forecasts, clues, reports from volunteers, and any investigative results. He then conferred with his staff, accepting input from experienced wardens such as Scott Thrasher, Brock Clukey, Investigator Phil Dugas, and others.

Wherever the teams were deployed, the terrain posed a problem. At certain elevations, the forest surrounding this portion of the Appalachian Trail is so thick it is impossible to see a person standing five feet from you. Sometimes you cannot see your own feet. For perspective, the most difficult forest terrain in Montana, Idaho, and Wyoming is a cakewalk compared to some of the backcountry in northern Maine. It can be hard to convey the difficulty of trying to navigate the North Maine Woods to those who don't have the experience. Sadly, one need only consult Appalachian Trail forums on the internet to realize how serially underestimated the task is; many former thru-hikers insist that carrying a compass is "not necessary," advising prospective hikers to "just stay on the trail."

In the long hours that Gerry waited, isolated from the rest of the world, she kept her chin up the best she could. She read and reread Terry Bliss's blog and said her rosary. And she waited.

Gerry tried several more times to signal search planes. She tried again to light fire to different dead spruce logs just north of her tent. She lit pine needles and twigs next to the fallen logs where they lay on the forest floor. The needles caught, and so did the twigs. The flames lapped at the logs and even burned for a few moments, but the insides of the logs were moist, and the flames always went out. She finally did get some small fires to take, but when she was sure the aircraft was gone, she put the small fires out. She no doubt was in the depths of despair.

CHAPTER ELEVEN

Dig Deeper, Keep Looking

Everybody on that mountain wanted Gerry found. Everybody.
—LIEUTENANT COMMANDER J. D. WALKER, US NAVY (RET.)

When the fires did not help, Gerry did the only thing else she knew to do: She waited. *If lost, stay put*, she had heard people say. The problem was that she had dug herself into some of the most difficult terrain in the area. She had hiked up instead of downhill. In the mountains—especially when there are numerous steep ridges, valleys, arroyos, and peaks—the wind does odd things. It can even sound like voices. Also, the mountains make their own climate. The wind swirls and twists through the ridge-lines. It will waft over a peak and become impacted between the summit of the ridge and other air currents above, increasing velocity, like when you place your thumb over the nozzle of a garden hose. Typically, it mixes with the cooler air and settles in the low spots of the valleys. In the undulating ridges all around Gerry's campsite, the wind wreaked havoc on the K-9 units looking for her. Also, Gerry had set her camp in such a remote place that the dog teams would have to be cast from miles away before they could even start their search.

Maine Search and Rescue Dogs (MESARD) sent multiple team members to work the area with their K-9s within a mile of Gerry. Deb Palman, a Maine institution herself, knew the terrain would not be easy for the dogs. A retired game warden for the state of Maine, Palman is, in fact, the only woman to have worked her entire career in the service as an active game warden. Before retiring, she was training coordinator for the Maine Warden Service K-9 Team and is one of the founding members of MESARD.

Dogs have become an important part of the search-and-rescue community in Maine. When Lieutenant Adam mobilizes his search teams, K-9s and their handlers are often the first resource called. Local and state police K-9 teams sometimes respond to the call. As Palman reports in one of her many articles for the SAR community, "If the local police K-9 is a good tracking dog, or if he/she gets an easy track, they are able to locate the lost person. More often, the police K-9 is not trained in scent discrimination, or SAR type tracks and the dog will track the family members who have already been searching or start the correct track and lose it along the way." Utilizing a dog on a relatively short, "aggressive mode search" for a fleeing criminal is very different from trying to search a vast area for a lost person. "Sometimes [police] patrol K-9s that have not had training in scent search and rescue will attempt to search for lost persons by search 'off-lead.' If the terrain is open and the handler can see the dog most of the time, this often works, but I know of many horror stories where police patrol dog teams failed to locate unresponsive subjects and left the area and 'cleared' it."

In Gerry's case, there were enough search and rescue–trained K-9 teams to clear many areas, one at a time.

Some of the K-9 search teams drove more than four hours just to get to the Rangeley area. They rented cabins or motel rooms. Once at the motels, the actual search area was so remote that it took hours to get the dog teams in place.

"There were six to seven MESARD dog teams involved in the search, plus some state police cadaver dog teams," recounts Palman. "Some teams drove as close as they could and hiked in the rest of the way, and some were transported by way of tote roads on ATVs. Often, by the time we were able to search, it was midday. We were supposed to be out of the woods by 5:00 [p.m.]."

Palman explained that by midday—especially in the summer—there is often a "knoll effect," in which "the tops of the ridges and knolls heat up first, and any scent that might be there raises up. It gets transported by the wind, and, since we know cool air settles, the scent gets deposited into ravines and valleys sometimes miles away."

In the earliest days of the search, there were "hits" with the dogs all along southern and western slopes of Mount Abraham (not to be confused with nearby Mount Abram) more than two miles from where Gerry was waiting—holed up in her tent, praying to be rescued. The topography compounded the difficulties of the swirling winds and the knoll effect. "The terrain was just *so* bad," Palman remembers. "Even the dogs had a look in their eyes like 'Are you kidding me?' Movement in the undergrowth was so difficult to negotiate, on a few occasions we had to carry our dogs."

Some news reports suggested that any scent from Gerry's site may have been inhibited by her being holed-up in her sleeping bag, in her zipped-up nylon tent. That is unlikely. It is more probable that the knoll effect deposited any scents in places far remote from her campsite.

The hours turned into days, and, except for getting water periodically and trying to start signal fires and making noise, Gerry had nothing else to do besides write in her journal and reread what little material she had. She spent a great deal of time in her sleeping bag.

In my twenties, at the peak of my climbing career, I was afflicted with altitude sickness above twenty thousand feet. It was made worse when I contracted pulmonary edema. I was very sick. We descended quickly (our lowest camp was at fourteen thousand feet). I was given medical attention and support. I stayed at that base camp for two days, sleeping for one to three hours at a time, before I could walk out of the mountains. By the time we got out of base camp—four days after the descent from the mountain—I was sure that I had been in that tent for more than a week. I was convinced at least nine days had gone by since I'd gotten sick. Time can be confounding, stuck in a tent with dwindling cognition.

Donn Fendler experienced hallucinations on his second day lost in the woods of Maine.

Exhausted from worry and stress, Gerry would have catnapped both at night and in the daytime. Sleeping periodically would have made her unaware of the time. She had a timepiece, but in her mind, the *days* would be increasingly hard to keep track of.

On Tuesday morning, July 30, Gerry again heard an airplane overhead. She couldn't tell how far away it was, but she waved her red fleece jacket—the same red jacket she was wearing in the photo Dottie took of her at Poplar Ridge Lean-To—and tried in vain to signal the plane. Later she heard a helicopter. Again, she tried to signal the aircraft. The pilot couldn't see her.

That same day, eight days after Gerry had stepped off the AT, the major search effort was still under way, but the wardens and volunteers were feeling a sense of urgency and frustration. The methodic, routine search-and-rescue techniques and protocols were still being followed. Because no hard clues of Gerry's whereabouts had been discovered—it was now days beyond the initial twenty-four hours, the time in which, statistics tell us, 97 percent of lost people are found—collectively the warden's professionalism was becoming tinted with desperation.

Each afternoon, Lieutenant Adam would try to organize all the pieces of the puzzle: the reports from the K-9 teams and volunteers, his wardens, and the navy's SERE searchers; the testimony from George; the bits of information filtering into the Warden Service from Appalachian Trail hikers; the point last seen; and input from countless other people and agencies. He moved the puzzle pieces around, first in his mind, then on the maps, and tried to make them fit together. Some of the pieces snapped in place nicely—all the normal search-and-rescue techniques were being used—but the large vacant spots in the puzzle, in some of the roughest terrain in the northeast, were disconcerting. There are places in Maine just off the Appalachian Trail where a body can slip into large cracks and deep, dark holes between the huge granite slabs that were smashed together ten thousand years ago by glaciers. Now, more than a week after Gerry's disappearance, Adam feared the worst. *Where did you go, Gerry?*

The whole state of Maine seemed worried about *Inchworm*. Dozens of people telephoned the Warden Service and the state police offering help. From nearby villages like Perham and East Madrid, farmers, woodsmen, and crusty old men who seem to be modern-day hunter-gatherers hit the old logging trails on their ATVs and on foot. Folk who know the woods there better than anyone searched entirely on their own.

At the SERE school, only a mile or so from where Gerry was camped, Lieutenant Commander J. D. Walker's contractors continued to search for Gerry. He wanted to search for her himself but knew that would be impossible. Many of the men under his command, men like Dennis Haug, are search and rescue trained and experts in survival. Walker encouraged them all to look for Gerry when not actively teaching and supervising students.

Scores of volunteers showed up to the search area every day, bashing their way through the obtrusive "puckerbrush" (as the thick undergrowth is called in Maine), climbing over and peering down into deep fissures between vertical slabs of granite the size of houses, and fording the many brooks that drain the steep ravines. "We were very lucky that no volunteers were seriously hurt," Lieutenant Adam said later.

Gerry, meanwhile, simply waited at her campsite, striving to assuage her anguish with prayer.

By this point, the AT community was collectively beside itself. Most Appalachian Trail hikers—especially thru-hikers—cherish a special bond acquired on the trail. It is a sense of community that reflects a kind of brotherhood or sisterhood. A thru-hike endured is something shared in that community, no matter if the individual's hikes are decades apart. Many thru-hikers today still share a bond with Emma "Grandma" Gatewood, who died in 1973. Now, forty years later, one of their sisters was missing.

At every trail and road crossing for forty miles along the Appalachian Trail, the Maine game warden had hung missing posters where it could be seen by both north- and southbound hikers. There was her description: *5'5", Age: 66, 115 Pounds* . . . and of course there was Dottie Rust's photograph—Gerry standing in front of Poplar Ridge Lean-To more than a week earlier, snapping her pack's waist belt, her contagious smile flashing for every worried soul to see.

Gerry read and reread the small printed section of Terry Bliss's Appalachian Trail blog. She kept what little reading and writing material she had in a Ziploc bag. On the night of July 27, 159 miles north, at White House Landing on the western tip of Pemadumcook Lake, Terry

Blue Moon Bliss first heard the news about *Inchworm*, with whom he had passed the time on her first night as a solo hiker more than a month earlier in New Hampshire. He was shocked. Terry could do nothing where he was.

"It was very frustrating," recalls Terry. "I felt anxious. I thought about turning around and hiking back to help look for her, but I was so many miles away . . . I would be too late. So I kept going. But I thought about her a *lot*." He rolled around in his mind the pleasant conversations he'd had with Gerry—about their families, hiking, and careers. "I even remembered the foot powder we both used."

"I remember thinking about her that night while I tried to sleep," said Terry, "and thinking about how the trail is so much tougher in Maine."

Terry wouldn't find out until 2017 that a printout of his blog had been one of the few pieces of reading material she'd had with her in her last days.

Bobby *Kermit* Thompson—who'd told Gerry back on June 3 that "happiness is solar-powered"—also learned *Inchworm* had gone missing. At first, he regretted having encouraged Gerry to keep going that day on the steps of Zealand Falls Hut, when she'd been thinking about quitting because of the rain. But the more he thought about it, the more his regret abated, though the sadness did not. "Like my dad and me, she was pursuing her dream. Not everyone gets to do that," said Bobby.

Gerry, waiting in her tent, less than three thousand feet from the Appalachian Trail, likely had no idea how profoundly she had affected so many people she had met. Friendship is the very stuff of life, and Gerry engaged people everywhere she went. Dottie Rust and Regina Clark, who had spent the night with her before she became lost—two tough, accomplished professional women and athletes—were devastated. Five days after they had finished their southbound section hike, they were home in Maryland, back at work. Coincidentally, it was five days since they had said goodbye to Gerry at the Poplar Ridge shelter that Paul Renaud called Dottie from the Appalachian Trail Lodge to inquire about Gerry. Now Regina and Dottie both were consumed with thoughts of *Inchworm*.

Mary *Tenderfoot* Blanton—at whose home George, Gerry, and Jane had spent their few zero days in Vermont—was hiking south through the Hundred-Mile Wilderness when she saw one of the warden's posters. It stopped her dead in her tracks. "I had been looking forward to meeting her again on the trail," recalls Mary. "I had cell service and immediately called George. It had been a week, and she hadn't been found. I had planned to hike all the way back to Vermont, but all my desire to hike flowed out of me, and fear that there might have been foul play made me think I shouldn't hike the section where she went missing." Mary continued her section hike for a few more miles. Then, feeling despondent over Gerry—and fearful—she left the trail in Caratunk and quit. She would return for that section the next year.

Tim *Walker* McElhannon, a much faster hiker, was miles ahead of Gerry and just about to enter the Hundred-Mile Wilderness when he heard of her disappearance. "I was very upset and called my wife to let her know about Gerry," recalls Tim. "I thought of going back to Rangeley and getting involved with the search but decided I might be more of a hindrance than help." Tim is an ex-navy helicopter pilot, trained in navigation, and had years before been through the navy's SERE training program at the same facility in Maine near where Gerry had gone missing. But he understood from his navy experience that the search effort would be, in his words, "better left to those who are properly trained."

"Because *Inchworm* was such a memorable person on the trail," remembers Tim, "there was a *lot* of discussion about her among hikers." Some suspected foul play; others thought perhaps she had gone missing on purpose—dropped out and simply left the trail and vamoosed for whatever reason. Tim remembers clearly, "I was absolutely sure that she had not purposefully gone missing. She had too much to live for; she was happy."

Like many others, Tim couldn't stop thinking of her. He thought about the time he had spent with her and with George just before she'd stepped off the trail and gotten lost. He thought about the ice cream he'd had with George in Rangeley. He thought about the pizza he'd eaten with them both two nights before she'd left Poplar Ridge. He thought about all the discussions they'd had—leaving Atlanta, resettling in the Nashville area, their reasons for hiking, and Gerry and George wanting to be near their grandchildren, "her babies." And he thought about the last time he'd seen them on the trail on the way into Poplar Ridge, the day before she'd gone missing, how their demeanor was different. He remembered how they hadn't been as warm and friendly as the night before. Tim had known it was none of his business and had hugged them both goodbye. Still, he couldn't help but wonder whether they were "having an argument or something." Tim clung to the warm memories of *Inchworm* and George, but that single out-of-sorts encounter on the trail into Poplar Ridge haunted him for a long time.

More than a hundred tips were called in over the first five months after Gerry had gone missing. I've asked many law enforcement folks what percentage of the tips they would guess turn out to be helpful, but most wouldn't hazard a guess. "Not many," said one officer, after giving the question some thought. "Maybe 2 percent," said another, adding, "but we *really* need those 2 percent, so we're obliged to look at every tip that comes in."

Gerry's case was no different. The tips and offers to help came in from seemingly everywhere. The wardens wanted to hear from her friends, family, and hikers who had either hiked with her on the trail or seen her. Piecing the puzzle together became more difficult for Lieutenant Adam as time went on because of the mistaken or unsure identities. The hiker who'd called the Stratton Motel three days after *Inchworm* had gone missing, it turned out, had *not* shared the Spaulding Mountain Lean-To with Gerry—and had never said that she had. Five days after getting the call, in the sea of Appalachian Trail hikers, the wardens, armed only with a trail name, finally tracked down the caller (whose real name turned out to be Kathy) on the trail miles to the north. There had been some confusion in the hand-off of information between the hotel and the Warden Service. Misinformation is common, especially these days when communication is instantaneously at everyone's fingertips. It is not necessarily egregious. In Gerry's case, people from every direction of the compass had simply wanted to help. The caller, *Kaleidoscope*, did not look much like Gerry but fit the bill enough that she told one journalist, "One day on the trail at least twelve people asked me if I was *Inchworm*."

When the wardens interviewed the three teenage southbound hikers on the third day of the search, Dottie Rust did not yet know Gerry was missing, and so the wardens did not yet have her photograph from Poplar Ridge to show the boys. The woman the boys had seen on the AT below Lone Mountain fitting *Inchworm*'s description turned out to be the taciturn hiker *Ivanich*, who had spent the night with Regina Clark, Dottie Rust, and Gerry at the Poplar Ridge shelter the night before she'd became lost. The boys had never been able to say for certain that the woman they'd seen was *Inchworm*. They had also stayed on and tried to help in any way they could.

It is remarkable how many people called the Warden Service wanting only to talk to a warden or an investigator. Some had pieced together snippets from news reports and had formulated their ideas about where Gerry was. Others wanted to discuss their own experiences on the trail, even experiences from years prior. Some had sustained injuries and wanted the searchers to know how precarious the terrain is. The wardens are acutely aware of the difficulties, but just in case there might be something—*anything*—useful, they read all the messages and followed up on each call. One hiker wrote a letter recounting her trek in the Rangeley area ten years earlier. On that hike, she had been caught in heavy wind and forced off the mountain. She wanted the wardens to check the treetops.

There were more than a dozen hiker concerns conveyed to the investigators regarding a male hiker with the trail name *Navigator*. He had left his mark by purposefully leaving Jolly Rancher candy wrappers on the trail and in shelters. All the calls were from female hikers who felt nervous about his behavior—even threatened. Investigators checked him out. *Navigator* was guilty of littering, certainly, but beyond that his only offense was creeping out the women.

Many of the theories e-mailed or called in to the authorities were born on several of the online Appalachian Trail forums. The forums are a wealth of information, and members are quite happy to help fellow hikers at the drop of a hat. But in *Inchworm*'s case, thousands of posts fueled scores of theories about her fate based on assumptions and passion, some of which were hurtful to Gerry's friends. One of the common threads that had leaked from somewhere was that Gerry had been known to use lorazepam—a benzodiazepine medication used by millions of people for a variety of reasons, including helping with seizures, providing mild sedation, and preventing anxiety. The forums were rife with pontifications about the medication suggesting it had been a contributing factor in her disappearance—or was at least why she hadn't yet been found.

The wardens knew about Gerry's "as needed" prescription. They had conferred with the prescribing physician and dismissed the history as irrelevant. "That was good enough for me," recalls Jane Lee, who knew Gerry's habits while on the trail better than anyone. She agreed with the wardens: "It was a nonissue!" Jane insists.

At a base level, the people on the forum were genuinely concerned. *Inchworm* was one of them, after all. They all wanted her home safely. Hundreds of people seemed to know what her problem was and what had happened to her. But no one knew where she was.

By the afternoon of Tuesday, July 30, Lieutenant Adam briefed Gerry's family, nearly all of whom had been at the command center for several days. The major search was to be postponed. Warden Investigator Joshua Bubier took inventory of George's Toyota Highlander. Besides a DeLorme gazetteer, there was the official Appalachian Trail guide to Maine, an *Appalachian Trail Data Book*, a roadmap, and Gerry's trail journal.

"When a search doesn't go favorably, telling families is the most important part of my job," Lieutenant Kevin Adam said in 2018. Staring at a spot in the woodwork of the table where he was sitting, he said, "You just try to stay as professional and as unemotional as you can. It can be tough. You can't attempt to eliminate their anguish, but you can continue to support them—you can let them know you'll still be there to help them."

On Thursday, August 1, eleven days after Gerry had gone missing, Warden Scott Stevens, accompanied by George and a friend from Nashville, acted on a lead from a hiker named Randy. The hiker had said two days earlier that, while crossing the rim of the steep bowl on the Sugarloaf summit trail, he thought he heard someone moaning "down over the rim of the bowl." He may have, but it wasn't Gerry. The men walked along the rim of the bowl, blowing whistles. Almost six miles away as the crow flies, Gerry also was likely blowing her small whistle that had been attached to the shoulder strap of her backpack.

Lieutenant Adam and his team revised their plan. There would be one more major search effort on the following Sunday, August 4. In the meantime, twenty-four hours after postponing the major search, Lieutenant Adam, Sergeant Scott Thrasher, Investigator Phil Dugas, and Wardens Kris MacCabe and Scott Stevens hiked the eight-mile section of the Appalachian Trail from Lone Mountain to Caribou Pond Road in 80 percent humidity. They could not give up. They hoped that Gerry was still alive. She was.

Before sunup that same morning, the incident command center on Sugarloaf Mountain was already accumulating searchers. The push was on. Approximately 115 people were on hand, made up of the Warden Service's Incident Management Team—led by Lieutenant Adam—twenty-three game wardens, state police, MASAR volunteer search groups, MESARD K-9 teams, Maine Forest Service, and US Border Patrol agents. Armed with the knowledge that the three teenagers had seen northbound hiker *Ivanich* and not *Inchworm*, and that the call made to the Stratton Motel had been misconstrued, the teams focused on all of the unsearched (or less searched) areas between Orbeton Stream and Lone Mountain. They had figured it out: many of the searchers were within two miles of Gerry (some were even closer). But the main problem—the terrain—had not changed in the past thirteen days. Getting crews from the command center—from *anywhere*—was difficult. Teams often had to be shuttled by ATVs to jumping-off spots to initiate their searches. The forest and topography of the mountainous terrain where Gerry lay waiting was so difficult that Lieutenant Adam could only send his most experienced, fittest searchers. If he sent scores of people in the area north-northwest of Redington Pond, chances were good that he would have to divert many of his crew to haul out injured searchers.

Dennis Haug and his navy comrades were still devoting every spare moment searching their SERE property along the border with the

Appalachian Trail corridor. At times, they would meet other nonmilitary rescuers deep in the woods. The navy contractors were still keeping in touch with the wardens' command center through their base on the SERE property.

Dennis remembers it as though it were yesterday: "We descended from the northwest, off two no-named mountains, and followed the drainages southwest toward the Railroad Road and Orbeton Stream. We picked up a small brook and hiked downstream. We didn't hear anything or see anything that day."

Most of the wardens who reported to the search that Sunday had worked all week, day and night, in their respective districts. Some had driven two hundred miles to the search area. The wardens were tired—running on fumes.

That day, August 4, the game wardens alone logged 294 hours, with 265.5 overtime hours. By truck, ATV, and foot, they covered 6,656 miles. That's the distance from Monson, Maine, to Xinjiang, China, with a few miles left over for sightseeing. There was no sign whatsoever of *Inchworm*.

On August 5, twelve days into the search, Lieutenant Adam suggested to George Largay, his daughter, Kerry, and Kerry's husband, Ryan, that they all return home. He would not stop searching and would keep them updated.

Before Gerry's family drove back to their homes in Tennessee, they stood by the side of the road holding handmade signs, thanking the volunteers and the people of Maine. George and a friend stayed a bit longer, helping and hoping. Meanwhile, every lead would be tracked down. Search flights were planned for November, when the leaves would have fallen off the trees. Perhaps they would find the answer. On the ground, wardens would still beat the bushes.

The next day, there was a debriefing at the command center. The day after that, Lieutenant Adam closed up the mobile command vehicle and transported it back the ninety-six miles to Greenville, Maine, where he is based. He was not happy.

Chapter Twelve

Acquiescence

We shall stick it out to the end, but we are getting weaker, of course, and the end cannot be far. It seems a pity, but I do not think I can write more.

—Robert Falcon Scott

Gerry's tent, propped on top of the highest ridge around, set up under a hemlock tree on a thin platform of twigs and sticks, pine needles and leaves, became the heart of her world. Her love of family and friends, her faith and dreams, remained the soul of it.

By day eight of her ordeal, Gerry would have known she was in real trouble. After careful rationing, she had been deprived of any calories for days. By day eight, she knew. She wrote stoic, heartfelt entries in her journal. She tried to prepare herself for the worst. But, still, her faith never left her.

Depending on environmental conditions, most people believe they can survive without water for three days and without food (and zero caloric intake) for three weeks, but there are so many contributing factors, I don't go by it. History is rife with cases of people soldiering on and living far beyond those limits. People have lived for a week to ten days without water—providing they're not in an environment like the Sahara. Without food, depending on how fat (or fit) they were to begin with, and how well hydrated they are, death can occur in about thirty to forty days on average. Some hardy souls have lived much longer.

Throughout history, there are numerous accounts of individuals who survived starvation: the previously mentioned John Franklin, for example. In 1819, twenty-six years before his ill-fated Arctic expedition, Sir John had led a small party of a few Brits, great Scottish naturalist and naval surgeon John Richardson, some voyageurs, and a half dozen "Indians" overland from Hudson Bay northward to map and survey the coast of the North Polar Sea. As often happened in British expeditions of the day, they woefully misjudged the difficulties, conditions, and provisions required. With their stores depleted and in retreat from the north, the party lasted eight months eating lichen and boiled shoe leather. Most of them lived, but only after a murder, an execution, and probably some cannibalism by some of the voyageurs. There are numerous other stories of people living many weeks in the throes of starvation. A number of factors contribute to survival without food: mental awareness, faith, conditioning, the cold, the heat, how one copes with the stressors of being lost and hungry, water intake, the will to live . . . hope. It's needless to speculate on how long *Inchworm* might have lived without calories. It is merely conjecture and beyond any lessons Gerry's ordeal can offer future hikers.

Though authorities had quickly dismissed any notions that George had a hand in her disappearance, the lack of any evidence or any signs of Gerry meant investigators could not dismiss foul play completely. The not knowing was taxing for the family.

In the absence of any sign, and taking into account the bad tip called in to the Stratton Motel *and* the three teenage boys' inability to identify with certainty the woman hiker they had seen on the trail between Orbeton Stream and Spaulding Mountain, Lieutenant Adam and his team were still assessing lost-person behavior in their search for *Inchworm* long after the point when lost hikers are typically found.

During most searches for missing persons that receive national attention, clairvoyants and psychics enter the fray. It's as though they can't help themselves. The higher the profile of the case, the more psychics call. If it's a particularly heart-wrenching case or an egregious crime, investigators may pay more attention to the tips. Calls from psychics are not referred to as *leads*. Since every tip or lead is investigated, police will often follow up on a psychic's input to make sure the caller is not actually a person involved in the case—or even a possible criminal. But more often than not, the hope for the investigator is that some interesting or important piece of information might be gleaned from the call. Typically, however, what is offered are general, imprecise, commonsensical statements that aren't all that helpful.

The FBI tries to fly under the public's radar, yet is high profile by nature, and so it gets its fair share of input from psychics. I contacted police agencies from five states (including California) and the FBI about this, and all said essentially the same thing: they welcome the input, but everyone I spoke with was unaware of any investigations that had significantly progressed solely by information provided by a psychic medium.

However, some police agencies don't rule out the use of psychics. Most police agencies (if they're interested) ask mediums and psychics for references. The person's methods should be asked for and whether they have any "accredited successes," according to a consultation document from the College of Policing, the official arbiter of professional practice on police work in the United Kingdom.

Here in the States, a small percentage of police agencies have historically included psychics in their investigations, but more often in recovery scenarios. In Maine, the larger police agencies all seem to have a simple approach to handling information called in by psychics: each agency I contacted stated that they "welcome any information from people who feel they are able to assist."

On July 30, ten days after Gerry became lost, the first psychic called, and she happened to be from Maine (Mainers are a pragmatic lot, born of an agrarian culture, and there are relatively few psychics there). She had seen Gerry's missing-person photo posted on Facebook, she claimed. "The woman had lost her footing," the psychic said, "and she's trapped in a ditch." She also "felt" a moose and a river near Gerry. Also, she also saw a guardrail "that was bearing off to the left, then straight—and a covered bridge. She is in that area." The closest covered bridge to where Gerry went missing is more than thirty miles away, in Lincoln Plantation—"clear over to the New Hampshire border," as they say in Maine.

On August 18, a medium from New York called. She had a long list of cases she'd participated in, along with references, and claimed to have worked with the FBI, adding that she is "accurate in her visions, and . . . very successful." She said that she "sensed Gerry had fallen and had head and rib injuries." She also sensed "the numbers two and twenty-six, which could be in relation to miles in which she was last seen." The medium told the warden investigator that she had used a pendulum over a map and "got" a latitude and longitude. The investigator checked the coordinates. It was in an empty lot in the town of Wilton, Maine—also thirty miles away from where Gerry actually was and in the opposite direction from the location offered by the first psychic. This second medium said her friend had also used the pendulum and then relayed the new set of coordinates. Again the investigators checked them out, and this time the location was in the deep rough, behind the fifth tee at Prospect Hill Golf Course in Auburn, Maine.

One man called from North Carolina to say he'd had a vision that Gerry was off to the left of the trail by Long Mountain, with her backpack on and not alive.

Another caller, stating that she was a psychic, said, "Gerry is three miles from her destination to the left of the trail. She twisted her ankle and 'fell down the hill.' She was having memory lapses." The psychic asked the wardens to ask Gerry's husband about memory lapses. "She's not alive," said the psychic. "She's been taken by bobcats." Gerry's destination was Mount Katahdin, so the caller's directions were a bit vague. The wardens weren't too concerned about the bobcat statement. There hasn't been a single verified recorded death of an adult human from a bobcat attack in the entire state of Maine—or in the world.

On October 18, a different fellow called from North Carolina and said he had experienced "visions" only half a dozen times in his life and had been correct four times. He said Gerry was near a large rock that "kind of looks like a chimney" and her backpack was still with her. He told the investigators he could come up and find her. He was advised to call if he decided to come up to Maine.

Two days later, he called back. He quite confidently reported, "The missing hiker along the Appalachian trail can be located down a trail one mile from the point where she last phoned her husband. She will be about five hundred feet to the right, off the trail near a big rock with her backpack on or near her." He continued, "She did not make the river."

The caller told the wardens that he did not know how he knew this but reiterated that he had been correct about four past incidents involving missing persons. He left investigators with a final thought: "I feel she was forced off the trail."

A month later, the Warden Service received a typed letter from a woman in Tennessee addressed to spokesperson Corporal John Mac-Donald. "I am a professional psychic, and I am offering to help my fellow Tennessean Geraldine Largay," the letter said. "I am sure this may seem strange or unusual to you, or I assume, but I have helped law enforcement in many areas of the country and with great success." The psychic stated that she neither needed nor desired to travel to Maine and wasn't looking for fame or notoriety. She also sought no financial gains. "It would be nice," she wrote, "but to date I have not ever been paid to help. I would need a topo map of the area. I think you need to look where there are bluffs, caves, and water." There are no real cave systems known in Maine, but the entire western part of the state can be considered bluffs, and about 13 percent of the state is under water.

At the end of the letter, handwritten as almost an afterthought, she wrote, "I think the husband did her in."

Accusations such as those can be hard to take. One must be concerned about the wasted resources of police departments who expend precious time and human activity in following up on a psychic's meaningless "clues."

According to the Committee for Skeptical Inquiry (CSI), psychics often use a technique called "retrofitting," offering predictions that usually cannot be verified until the investigation has come to a conclusion. CSI is a nonprofit educational organization whose purpose is to "promote scientific inquiry, critical investigation, and the use of reason in examining controversial and extraordinary claims." They seek to investigate and debunk certain paranormal activity.

Whether one believes the legitimacy of psychics or not, they have always been available and probably always will. For the families of missing persons, a psychic's claims may give hope—either of finding their loved one or in the form of closure. Confirmation bias, the tendency to seek, interpret, or recall information in a way that confirms one's preexisting beliefs, can be a powerful thing. So can wishful thinking.

The day after Lieutenant Adam had returned the mobile command vehicle to Greenville, the search for Gerry continued, but on a smaller scale. On August 7, more than two weeks after Gerry had gone missing, Warden Scott Stevens, along with two Maine State Police detectives and two detectives from the Franklin County Sheriff's Office, hiked from where the AT crosses Perham Stream, up Lone Mountain, to Spaulding Mountain Lean-To. They conducted some grid searches but turned up nothing. At one point, they may have been within a mile of Gerry. Three days later, Lieutenant Adam was "back in the woods," with wardens Bubier, Thrasher, Clukey, and Christianson. They searched with some MESARD K-9 teams from Lone Mountain to nearby Mount Abraham.

Every three or four days for the rest of August, the wardens conducted searches between Poplar Ridge Lean-To and Spaulding Mountain Lean-To. The only thing found was a trekking pole, but it was a Leki brand; Gerry had Black Diamond Trail Pro Shock poles. Retired warden Deb Palman and her dog and other MESARD K-9 units, amid the swirling winds, continued to search the rugged area north of Redington Pond, paralleling the Appalachian Trail corridor and the navy's SERE property. At one point in mid-August, one of the dogs indicated interest along one of the small brooks that drains the east side of Mount Redington. (Looking at the GPS tracking map later downloaded from her phone, I believe it was the first brook Gerry had crossed while she was wandering that first day.) The wind changed quickly, and the dog lost interest. But the "alert" was very real to the handlers. Palman searched the area, as well as the terrain would allow with the personnel she had.

Wardens continued to search through the rest of August, especially with K-9 teams. As the summer inched toward its close, the search had become a recovery investigation rather than a rescue. Still, Lieutenant Adam kept working. On September 27, eleven wardens, four Warden Service and Maine State Police K-9 units, and a group of Mahoosuc

Mountain Search and Rescue Team volunteers conducted another search in the Redington AT corridor north of Redington Pond and onto the SERE property, and twelve of the volunteers searched on the south side of Orbeton Stream where other dog teams had earlier displayed an interest. Lieutenant Adam had narrowed his focus by early August, guided by the displays from the K-9 units and also because of the Warden Service's intense investigation. He eliminated all extraneous input. But the outcome was the same as all previous searches for *Inchworm*.

When Warden Scott Thrasher filed his official report that day, he succinctly wrote, "Mrs. Largay or anything belonging to her was not located."

While the massive search had been going on, sometimes less than a mile from where Gerry was camped—sometimes as close as six hundred yards—Gerry tried to hold fast. She prayed and said her rosary. The devout, during times of duress, will often cling to the simplest truths of their faith; the rosary begins with the Apostles' Creed—a summarization of the great mysteries of the Church of Rome. In the creed she would have found strength. She prayed for the safety of searchers, for the pilots of the planes she could hear in the distance, and for her family.

Gerry ate her last bit of rationed food by the sixth day. At one point, she considered moving her camp to a different site—perhaps to a more open space—but in the end decided not to. *Stay put*—she would have known that from her Girl Scout days. Yet she hadn't stayed put, not when it had mattered most. Not when she had first realized she was lost. She had thrashed and scrambled so far on her first day that she was now quite removed from her point last seen. And moving again would make her weak. She may have decided not to do so because she was already too weak.

During the following days, consuming no calories, Gerry tried to stay hydrated and tried to occupy her mind. She still practiced taking bearings with her tiny compass, walking from one tree to another, keeping her tent in sight. She reread a paperback novel she had brought along for this section of the hike and Terry Bliss's Appalachian Trail blog printout. She prayed some more.

On August 6, the same day Lieutenant Adam had packed up the incident command vehicle and moved it back to Greenville, Gerry powered up her phone and re-sent a text to George. Still no service. He did not get it.

When she had left the Poplar Ridge shelter fifteen days earlier, Gerry had been physically fit. One can see the physical transformation she underwent from the photographs taken over the span of her hike—from a relatively fit sixty-plus-year-old woman to the younger-looking, lean Appalachian Trail thru-hiker in Dottie Rust's photograph at Poplar Ridge. When Dottie snapped the photo of *Inchworm* leaving the shelter, Gerry had been on her AT odyssey for exactly ninety days. But no matter how fit Gerry was, no matter how well she had been hiking, the stress of finding herself lost would have taken its toll.

The strain of being hopelessly lost, or in some other life-threatening situation, is not simply an emotion. There is a profound physical response. When we're suddenly stressed, our hypothalamic-pituitary-adrenal axis—our central stress-response system—is activated and the body releases cortisol and adrenaline, hormones that cause our lungs to saturate our blood stream with extra oxygen quickly. It also increases our blood pressure. Tens of thousands of years ago, the extra oxygen saturation in the blood would have given us the burst of energy to help us outrun the stressor—perhaps a saber-toothed tiger or a jealous cavemate. One of the side effects is that the central response system uses up a lot of energy. The body stops repairing tissue. The constant cycle of debris-removing inflammatory cells, the formation of granulation tissue, and subsequent repair of connective tissue throughout the body are slowed. A chain reaction follows that includes an accelerated heart rate, increased glucose in the bloodstream, and the body's need for insulin to get the glucose out of the bloodstream and into the cells where it's needed, but the stress hormones make it difficult for the pancreas to secrete insulin. It is all very taxing on the body (it's part of that vagal response). When you're lost, the old recommendation is still best: *Stay calm.* Unfortunately, that's easier said than done.

Gerry surely felt the stress. As the days ticked by, she would eventually have become too weak to try to walk out on her own. Waiting in her tent, *Inchworm* had time to evaluate her life. Gazing back across the decades, she would have traded any adventure for some more time with her friends and family. Striving to erase her agony in prayer, and holding her closely woven world, defined by bonds of friendship, she undoubtedly longed for moments with her grandchildren—her "babies." In her journal, Gerry apologized to her family and assured them that no hike was as important as they were.

In one of her letters, she ended with "My deepest love to you, and to all my friends. I pray to see you all in heaven."

The very idea of someone struggling with starvation tugs at our heartstrings. Starvation is purely mechanical. Under normal conditions, the human body relies on free blood glucose as its primary energy source. When there is a severe deficiency in caloric energy intake, and the reserve stores of glycogen are exhausted, fatty acids become the principal metabolic fuel. After enough time, the energy source maintaining brain function is the body's proteins. The muscles begin to atrophy first, then the organs. Starvation follows when the fat reserves are completely exhausted and protein is the only fuel source available to the body. The loss of body protein affects the function of important organs. Death can result, even if there are still fat reserves left unused.

The leaner a person is, the earlier fat reserves are depleted. The protein depletion occurs sooner, and death can occur, usually from cardiac arrest following an arrhythmia caused by electrolyte imbalances. Atrophy of the stomach reduces the perception of hunger, since the perception is controlled by the percentage of the stomach that is empty. As a nurse, Gerry would have been aware of her atrophying arms and thighs. She would have been acutely cognizant of what was happening to her. As sweet as she was, she was a very tough person.

In the final stages of starvation, victims often experience a variety of psychiatric and neurological symptoms, including hallucinations, disturbances in the heart rhythm, and convulsions. There comes a point when you go into a state called Wernicke encephalopathy, in which you are still alive, semiconscious, but not exactly lucid. Knowing that, one wonders whether Gerry's journal dates are correct. Other symptoms accompany starvation, among them impulsivity and irritability. In the few journal entries read publicly, and from input from those who knew her well, Gerry, in the end, exhibited neither. Her writing near the end of her life was too elegant.

After more than two weeks of being lost, Gerry would have been aware that help might not come. She mentally prepared herself. She policed her campsite. One day, she cut up her credit card and buried the pieces, preventing anyone from finding it and potentially causing George problems.

When examining Gerry's life with her friends and hiking acquaintances, it becomes abundantly clear that she had always been considerate and always thought of others. She continued to do so, even facing death. She was concerned that her family would grieve deeper, mourn harder, not knowing what had happened to her. Sometimes the not knowing is the hardest part. That worried her.

On the same day that she tried to re-send her last text to George, Gerry wrote the following in her journal: *When you find my body, please call my husband George and my daughter Kerry. It will be the greatest kindness for them to know that I am dead and where you found me—no matter how many years from now. Please find it in your heart to mail the contents of this bag to one of them.*

She fastened the note to the cover of her journal and placed the bundle in a plastic baggie. The last two entries she wrote were dated August 10 and 18. Likely, she was confused about the dates as she faded.

In my life, I have been with far too many people as they died—people of all ages, religions, and genders. I held some in my arms. Hand on their chest, I felt their last breath. In more cases than not, there was a profound sense of grace—a dignity in their passing. Only once did I see someone fight hard at the very end. I do not know why.

Gerry was a Catholic. After centuries of ministering to the sick and dying, the Catholic Church has tremendous experience in what in the faith is called *ars moriendi*—the "art of dying." Centuries ago, Europe was still in social upheaval after the Black Death had ravaged the population. The *Ars Moriendi* are two related Latin texts, dating from about 1415 and 1450, that offer advice on the protocols and procedures of a good death, explaining how to "die well." The first edition was one of the first books printed with movable type and became extremely popular for the time, eventually being translated into most European languages.

The second version, printed around 1450, was shorter and included eleven woodcut pictures. It was printed as a "block book" (blocks of wood engraved with both text and illustrations). The engravings are considered a fine representation of medieval art. Some are pretty disturbing—with all the demons, little satanic creatures with pig's ears, beaks, and antennae, crowded around the deathbed. I tried to read a translation of the later, shorter edition but couldn't get through it, mostly because I could only find it in Old English, which is an arduous and tiresome language for the modern English speaker. I did find the engravings interesting. Some of the images are disturbing enough to encourage believers that they must live a good life or face hideous punishment after death among the frightful, hairy, horned pig people.

There are six chapters in the first edition. The first chapter explains that dying has a "good side" and attempts to console the dying man or woman by saying that death is not something to fear.

The second chapter outlines the five temptations that always torment a dying person and explains how to avoid them. These are lack of faith, despair, impatience, spiritual pride, and avarice. Apparently some things haven't changed since the Middle Ages. The temptations remain.

The third chapter lists the seven questions to ask a dying person, along with consolation available through the "redemptive powers of Christ's love." According to a Catholic priest I consulted, these questions are:

1. Do you believe fully in your chosen religion or lack thereof? Are you at peace with your choice?

2. Do you acknowledge all the sins you have committed? Be honest with yourself.

3. Are you sorry for them? Try to understand why they were wrong and find a way to forgive yourself for them.

4. How would you live differently if you were to live longer?

5. Can you forgive all the people who have hurt you, in words or actions? Reflect on what they have done or said, and find strength in your heart to let your pain and anger go.

6. Have you done your best to fulfill your responsibilities? If you have, you have nothing further to worry about; you have tried your best. If you haven't, you can still make arrangements so that they will be taken care of. You have to accept that you cannot personally fulfill these tasks and that it's okay. You are doing everything you can by finding the right people to take care of them for you, and that is all that's required of you.

7. Are you ready to let go of all your worldly and material possessions?

Pretty straightforward.

The fourth chapter enjoins the dying to imitate Christ's life, which seems a tad late. The fifth chapter addresses the friends and family of the dying, outlining the general rules of behavior at the deathbed. (Essentially, when the dying person can no longer speak on their own behalf, the attendants are to recite a series of prayers as they "commend the spirit of our brother" into God's hands.) The sixth chapter offers more official prayers for the dying.

Basically, the Church was encouraging people to die with dignity.

In 2016, I sat down and spoke with Father Frank Murray, whom I knew in high school. Father Frank was once the official clergy for the pediatric oncology department in Maine's largest medical center. We spoke about Gerry. "A common observance," he said, "is that people— even the very young—seem to find a certain peace. They go gently and embrace death."

Nearing the end, all that a sick and dying person can do is to exercise those virtues they have learned in life—through living.

Having seen in my life the strengthless will to live, and what human beings are capable of, I have confidence that Gerry lived for at least two weeks, and perhaps a few days longer, though I know others do not think so. By the way she lived her life, on and off the trail, she undoubtedly entered her house justified.

In September 2013, Jane Lee packed her car in Washington, D.C., and drove north. Like many people, she had not been able to stop thinking about Gerry. Jane wanted to be in Maine, and she wanted to be "hiking near her friend" on *Inchworm*'s birthday—September 10. The ground Gerry covered during her last day on the trail has become something akin to hallowed ground for those who knew her. Jane could no longer be with her friend, but she would go to her point last seen and hike that same section of trail. Closeness to her hiking partner was what she sought. Perhaps also answers. She wanted to "see what Gerry saw," she told the wardens later.

Jane hiked from Maine State Route 4 in Rangeley past Piazza Rock, past the spot where Tim McElhannon had met Gerry and George the day before she'd gone missing, and on to Poplar Ridge Lean-To. At the shelter, Jane found Jolly Rancher candy wrappers—undoubtedly from *Navigator*, the hiker known to litter them. Though the wardens had ruled the "creepy guy" out of any involvement in Gerry's disappearance, some hikers still wondered about foul play from some other source, even though such a thing is extremely rare in Maine. On a level spot a mile down the trail, Jane found three more wrappers. She traveled north, observing, wondering . . . reminiscing. The Appalachian Trail from Poplar Ridge to Orbeton Stream is just under three miles. The first half mile is quite a steep downhill grade. Some of the granite slabs are slick enough that Jane slid down on her bottom. She was sure Gerry would have had to do the same. Jane passed through the dark, thickly forested spot where, on July 21, Regina Clark had uncharacteristically stopped, turned to Dottie Rust, and said, "God, if you were six feet off the trail, you'd be a goner! Can't see anything in there." Jane continued on to Orbeton Stream. The water was low this late in the dry season, and she crossed it easily. If Gerry had lost her footing while fording it, Jane surmised, there would have been no place for her to go downstream; she would have been easily seen.

On the far side of the stream, Jane labored up over the very steep hundred feet of moss-covered boulders, the bared roots of tiny spruce trees clinging desperately to the granite slabs, and pulled herself up onto Railroad Road at the top. Jane looked down. *She surely could have fallen there*, she thought. *But, again, she would've been easily found.*

Jane rested for a moment on Railroad Road, just like Gerry probably had, and as most hikers do. *ATVs could use this road*, Jane thought. She couldn't have known then, but she was only a forty-minute walk through the woods from where Gerry's body lay. Jane was correct about the ATVs using the old railroad bed. In fact, it is a popular ATV trail and had been used almost daily during the search for *Inchworm*. At one point during the search, a short distance from where Jane now stood, it had been congested with a small village of camped volunteers. During the search, it had also been used as an access route for transporting K-9 units to their search areas—the handlers and dogs clinging to the backs of the ATVs.

Jane continued north on the AT, trekking along Sluice Brook as it parallels the trail, and then stepping from stone to stone across the tiny creek and beyond, to where a woods road crosses the trail on its way to some old cuttings on the lower slopes of Lone Mountain. She assessed the gravel woods road on either side of the trail. *I don't believe she got this far*, Jane thought. She hiked on another two miles to another old logging road where the trail crosses Perham Stream. Again, she carefully looked over the road. She wanted to know—she wanted to understand what the searchers were up against. She wanted to see the access points the wardens used. She wanted to feel the terrain under her feet. She wanted to know why her friend hadn't been found.

Jane lingered along the trail. She ate a leisurely breakfast during a break before reaching Lone Mountain, just as Gerry would have done had she made it this far. Jane wanted to be on a similar time line as her friend. All that she knew about Gerry as a hiking partner—her speed, habits, her desire to stay in shelters rather than her tent, her decision-making tendencies—contributed to her observations. In the end, Jane felt sure of only two things: that Gerry couldn't have fallen from the trail between Poplar Ridge and Spaulding Mountain Lean-To without being easily found, and

Gerry's time line between the two places. She found no answers. Silently, sadly, she wished Gerry a happy birthday.

In the absence of answers, Jane found something else on her quest, something wonderful: Below the bald summit of Saddleback Mountain, with its dwarf heath, evergreen shrubs, sedge, and highland rush, Jane heard a sound. It was the plaintive drone of bagpipes playing. She hiked past the pretty sound wafting from above her. Normally, she would have enjoyed the music in her own way and kept moving.

"But something told me to turn around and find this person," Jane remembers. "I followed the music. I found the guy, high on a cliff, and yelled up to him, thanking him for the beautiful music. I was moved.

"I yelled up to him that I was hiking for a dear friend of mine who was lost and that I was there to remember her on her birthday." There was an odd pause.

"Then the piper looked down over the cliff," recalls Jane.

He yelled down, "Jane . . . is that you?"

"I was shocked," says Jane. "Yes, my name is Jane." She was still digesting the moment. "He either had met me or knew of me."

The lone piper called down to Jane again: "There's a group of us . . . we're celebrating Gerry's life." There was a pause. "We have a birthday cake!"

Jane joined the group of friends. They all sang songs, ate cake, and cried for Gerry.

Warren Doyle called the Maine Warden Service again that September to talk to a detective. A few weeks after Gerry had gone missing, Doyle had been hiking in the Hundred-Mile Wilderness. He had been thinking of Gerry often. Everyone knew that foul play could not be ruled out at that point, and a recent experience had unnerved him.

"I was looking forward to camping on the eastern end of Nahmakanta Lake," recalls Doyle. "I was surprised when I got there that no one else was camped at the site."

After making a phone call from the beach, he was startled by a noise coming from behind him. (Doyle has a bearing that says he does not startle easily and doesn't fear much.)

"I turned around and saw a wiry, bespectacled man in his forties or fifties. He was wearing a button-down short-sleeve shirt and carrying a beat-up, old-style backpack. He was acting strangely and said, 'Do you have cell phone reception here?'"

"Yes . . . Verizon," replied Doyle.

"At that point," Doyle told the detective, "he just turned and headed down the shoreline. After about forty yards, he turned to see if anyone was watching. He reached into his pocket and threw a small object into the lake that reflected in the sunlight. I couldn't help but wonder: *Was that Gerry's cell phone?* I was so unnerved by the guy's behavior, I didn't stay."

Doyle took down the license plate and make and model of the only car in the parking lot and gave the information to the detective. A year later, Doyle was at the same spot and talked to the maintenance person assigned to the campsite. He told the man about the incident from the previous year.

"There was a squatter here last year," the maintenance man told him. "He had several knives on him. He was evicted from the site."

Throughout October 2013, in addition to tips, random calls were made to the Warden Service reporting items found by hikers along the Appalachian Trail. Even those that had been found far from the focus area of the search were investigated. None was Gerry's. As the long, gray, frigid winter descended onto Maine, case WS13-017786, Gerry's case, grew colder too. Throughout the fall and winter months, though the Warden Service had found every other person who had gotten lost in 2013, Lieutenant Adam often didn't sleep well. He had Gerry on his mind.

Calls continued to come into the Warden Service. Interestingly, among them were reports that Gerry had been seen in many places. In September, weeks after the major search had wound down, a woman called the wardens to report seeing Gerry in Cole Farms Restaurant in Gray, Maine, having a late lunch with an elderly man. The caller had seen

Gerry's picture in the newspapers and was certain it was her. She offered a description: "Didn't wear a bra, baggy pants, and was wearing hiking boots." The warden taking the call scribbled a note on the call sheet. "Not Geraldine!"

On September 8, another woman telephoned the Warden Service from Tennessee to report a conversation she'd had with an employee at an auto-auction company in Mount Juliet. The caller wanted the wardens to know that "the husband of the missing woman" had brought in his car for detailing and maintenance. Consider that George had just driven the Toyota Highlander over a thousand miles along the Appalachian National Scenic Trail, much of it on dirt roads and gravel parking lots. When confronted with a mystery, without answers, some people grow suspicious of, well, everything. "It still has camping equipment in the back," the caller said warily.

Then, in October, a woman faxed a note to the wardens, saying she thought "Gerry is at the Nashville Rescue Mission" on Rosa L. Parks Boulevard in that city. The woman had "seen her that morning." The wardens checked. She hadn't.

In December, a fellow from a popular Appalachian Trail forum wrote the Warden Service to report a post on his site. "Did the Maine Wardens ever check to see if there were any car rentals out of Rangeley at that time (during the search)?" the user had posted to the forum. "I ask because I had an older woman dressed in hiking clothes ask me to take a picture of her (using her camera) at Height of Land. Struck me odd, and actually commented to my family at that time that a hiker, dressed in hiking clothes, was driving a car." Height of Land is part of the thirty-two-mile Rangeley Lakes National Scenic Byway at the top of Spruce Mountain in Rangeley and is a popular vista for tourists. It is about eighteen miles south of where Gerry's campsite was. Again, not Gerry.

Just after New Year's in 2014, an interesting e-mail was sent to Warden Corporal John MacDonald from a woman in Rosemount, Minnesota. She had been holding a story in her heart for several weeks, she wrote, and could not let it go. "On December 12th," she wrote, "I walked into the Crystal Nail Salon in Edina Minnesota and noticed a woman getting her nails done that I thought I noticed. After about fifteen minutes of thinking 'who is that woman,' it dawned on me that she looked like Gerry Largay." The author of the e-mail had once worked for George in Minneapolis and had known Gerry well. But that had been twenty-five years earlier, and she had not been in contact with either Gerry or George since.

"As I sat deciding whether to say 'Hi' to her," the woman continued, "I Googled Gerry Largay out of curiosity on my iPhone and was absolutely shocked at what I found. I was truly sickened and stunned. The woman left the salon without me saying anything to her. I asked the technician if the woman's name was Gerry. She said no, and that she was a new customer that had started coming in two to three months ago. I showed her a picture of Gerry on my phone from the news reports, and she agreed that she looked just like the woman."

The woman said she "felt compelled to contact somebody with this information."

Within the State of Maine, the Warden Service or state police send one of their own or local law enforcement to follow up on tips and leads. For out-of-state tips, requests are sent to local authorities there. The woman in the salon checked out. But it was only another case of mistaken identity.

Seven days later, another e-mail arrived at the Maine Department of Inland Fisheries and Wildlife, with the subject line "Gerry Largay information." The body of the e-mail said, "Geraldine Largay possible sighting. I live in Massachusetts. The other day I was visiting a bookstore in Walpole Mass and I saw this lady that looked exactly like Geraldine Largay. She was 5'5", 110 pounds, black glasses, short black hair—in her mid-sixties. It looked like she had recently dyed her hair black. She was wearing a black and white backpack. She was with two small children. Just wondering if she had any connection with this area. I hope this was useful."

This tip was also pursued. But after the e-mail sender was further questioned, it was ruled out. Again, another false sighting.

As winter gave way to spring, Gerry's whereabouts never left the wardens' minds for long. Even at the end of May in the Redington range—especially on the north sides of the mountains—there can still be more than three feet of snow. Any more recovery searches would have to wait a bit longer.

Tips and calls from the public were still being addressed. Lieutenant Adam and Investigator Dugas stayed in touch with the Largay family.

In June 2014, almost a year after Gerry had gone missing, eleven wardens, some US Border Patrol agents, search-and-rescue volunteers from two teams, and MESARD K-9 units again searched the area from Orbeton Stream and up Railroad Road to the navy's SERE property. They then searched the forest between Orbeton Stream to the Poplar Ridge shelter. Finally, they revisited some of the logging roads to the north of Railroad Road. They had been there the previous August when some of the dog teams had displayed interest. Wardens Dave Chabot and Norm Lewis searched the Redington Pond Falls drainage. One team with a K-9 unit walked up the same terrain Dennis Haug and his navy search teams had traveled *down* while Gerry had possibly still been alive; the survival experts had banged on trees, yelled, and blown whistles to no avail.

Now, a year later, in the swirling, fickle breezes, they couldn't know it, but the wardens were no more than a few hundred yards from Gerry's campsite.

The very next day, there was a call into the Warden Service by a woman who believed the "missing AT hiker, Largay, may be staying with a camp owner in Monson," near the beginning of the Hundred-Mile Wilderness. Officer Bill Chandler drove to Monson and found the camp—and the AT hiker. Her name was Linda, and she was from Texas. She had been hiking the Appalachian Trail the previous summer and injured her head in a fall.

It wasn't until the fall of 2014, four days after what would have been Gerry's sixty-eighth birthday, that another recovery search was conducted, this time with sixteen wardens, plus teams made up of volunteers. They searched the south side of the AT, directly opposite where Gerry had actually left the trail. The north side had been scoured several times. Unfortunately, when the north side *had* been searched, the sixty searchers conducting it had only been able to cover the equivalent of a speck on the map of the vast woods of western Maine. One fact kept rearing its head: Gerry, while wandering in the first day after getting disoriented, had wandered too far from the point last seen—and from her cell phone ping. The country was just too big.

Another year went by. Nobody involved with the search forgot about Gerry.

In the autumn of 2015, one year and six days after the September 2014 search, another effort was made. Sixteen wardens answered the call, among them Lieutenant Adam, Brock Clukey, Kris MacCabe—men who had been involved with Gerry's case from the beginning. Warden Lewis's search dog, Clyde, who'd helped in earlier searches, was there again. Another 247 man-hours were spent looking for Gerry, not even including the volunteers' time, and 2,093 miles were covered by foot, truck, or ATV. Once again, no clue was found. The frustration was nearly palpable. By now the wardens knew: either Gerry had fallen into a crevice between two granite slabs, and was completely out of sight, or she had wandered too far into the forest and was too remote. She could've been anywhere in those thick, dark, cold, western Maine woods.

Perhaps the most distracting input from the public were the brewing conspiracy theories. They stirred emotions and ran the risk of being counterproductive. In June 2015, the *Bollard*, a small, locally owned alternative news source out of Portland, Maine, had published an article about Gerry under the headline, "M.I.A. ON THE A.T.: WHAT ROLE DID A COVERT NAVY 'TORTURE SCHOOL' PLAY IN THE DISAPPEARANCE OF GERALDINE LARGAY?" The *Bollard* is considered by many to be "citizen journalism"—the collection and analysis of information by the general public. Often, internet commentaries presented as "news" articles are simply blog pieces—opinions and pontifications unvetted by professional journalists. The *Bollard* article focused on a contrived theory regarding the navy's SERE school in the Redington Range. At the time it was written, it was already widely known—through her cell phone pings and the process of elimination—that Gerry had gotten lost very near the SERE property. The article called the SERE school a "secret military facility where trainees are left to fend for themselves in the woods, then hunted down and tortured in a mock prisoner-of-war camp." The *Bollard* called the contractors who teach survival and self-reliance at the school "soldiers of fortune." The folks at the *Bollard* wrote a compelling, sensational article, though I suspect none of them has been through the SERE program. The article was picked up by the online edition of the *Bangor Daily News*, a newspaper dedicated to being unbiased and asking the hard questions, in an effort to offer their readers an alternative point of view.

When the article came out, I was called by more than a dozen people asking me what I thought about it. So, I read it. I must say, it was well written, but the implication that some crazed student from the SERE program had stumbled upon a lost, sixty-six-year-old woman in the woods, freaked out, and possibly harmed her was too much for me.

"It's just a bunch of pernicious twaddle," I wrote back to one of my inquirers. "The rag is trying to generate traffic at their site," I said. *More power to them*, I thought at the time. I didn't believe anyone would take that line of thought seriously.

I was not surprised by the articles. In fact, I thought the author had brought up one interesting, legitimate point: because of the secrecy of— and restricted access to—the Redington naval facility, wasn't it possible that the area hadn't been searched as thoroughly as necessary? I did not yet have access to the official Maine Warden Service report of Gerry's case. Nobody had. Doug Comstock, my research assistant, had mentioned that very thing six months before the article came out. Studying maps of the area, he'd said, "How much communication had there been between the Warden Service and the navy's SERE school? Any? Were they searching the SERE property?"

It would be almost a year before we would get answers.

The *Bollard* published another article a year later, in July 2016, ten months after Gerry's campsite was finally discovered and her family had put the saga to rest. The authors were noticeably unapologetic for their previous 2015 article. In their follow-up piece, they also reached a bit further and rehashed the topic of her prescription medications, especially the lorazepam. The authors offered a litany of the worst possible side effects and withdrawal symptoms.

Most commonly used as a sedative for those with trouble sleeping, lorazepam is a good drug and helps millions of people around the world. Once it was mentioned in the *Bollard* article as a possible contributing factor for Gerry's predicament, the Appalachian Trail online forums lit up once again. Gerry had been hiking daily for months, covering more than nine hundred miles. It is unlikely she would have needed any sleep aid for some time. The wardens, of course, had investigated her medications thoroughly. After Lieutenant Adam spoke with George Largay, Jane Lee, and Gerry's prescribing physician about her medications, any serious withdrawal side effects from any of her meds was ruled a remote possibility but unlikely. Jane, invoking her registered-nurse credentials and familiarity with Gerry's routine after their intimate time hiking together, reiterated her view that the medication was not relevant to Gerry's disappearance. The bottom line was that even if she had still required occasional help sleeping, knowing this now would contribute little to finding her.

The *Bollard* article from 2016 suggested—based on the official 1,500-page case report released by the Maine Warden Service that May—"the documents contain evidence that strongly suggests Largay was experiencing dangerous withdrawal symptoms associated with the abrupt discontinuation of prescription anti-anxiety medication. Those symptoms, which are known to include panic attacks, depression, lethargy, confusion, memory problems, and even the loss of one's sense of identity or reality, likely explain why Largay apparently made little effort to signal her location to rescuers by building a campfire or blowing her emergency whistle."

While all those effects can and do happen with lorazepam use, close study of the warden's case report does not actually suggest any of that. There's no evidence that Gerry panicked. Did she become depressed about her situation? Most assuredly—as would most of us when facing our mortality. But from the few entries from Gerry's journal that have been made public, and from simply reading the graceful lines in the note to her would-be discoverer, it seems clear that her dignity and identity remained intact, even as she starved.

Were the theories in the *Bollard* impossible? Certainly not. Anything is possible, but we know now that Gerry's predicament was not pharmacological or born of foul play. It was physiological. It would have come down to three things: lost-person behavior, decision making (she did not know what to do if lost), and the effects of hunger and exposure—all of which were connected.

The *Bollard* articles served only as painful distractions for those who had beaten themselves up searching for Gerry. For Commander Walker at the SERE school, it was disconcerting. For the navy men and contractors who had searched so hard for her—sweating, bleeding, bug-bitten, and often working with no sleep—the articles were outright hurtful. *SERE students causing harm to someone?* They felt in their hearts such a thing could not happen. The US Navy usually takes a nonresponsive position, choosing to not engage with the "petty stuff," as one retired naval officer told me. "If something warrants a response," he said, "they will go through normal channels."

In 2016, Lieutenant Commander Walker, now retired, did offer one thought about the article: "To us, it was absurd," he told me. "It's mind-boggling how anyone can simply jump to such a different conclusion from something so straightforward."

It's probably mind-boggling to him because he was an officer—a former naval aviator. He is one of the many who sacrificed time, energy, and effort to serve his country. He would never say it, but as I listened to him talk with pride about his men who had searched for Gerry, I felt that collectively they would *like* to say their efforts should mean something and people should not jump to such conclusions. But, of course, he didn't. He did say that the men of DBAP (Don't Be a Problem) will continue to look for people who are lost.

When online citizen journalists such as those at the *Bollard* publish accusations like "the Navy made no concerted effort to find Largay" and "The tragic truth is that wardens did not receive assistance from the scores of physically fit SERE students and staff who were in that area during the height of the search effort" (July 4, 2016), it can ruffle some feathers. It considerably disturbed retired US Navy Senior Chief Dennis Haug. But not enough to respond to the allegations at the time the article came out. As my friend, a retired officer, told me, "The navy is resolute in their policy to not engage antipathy with a war of words. That's not our job."

Now that he was retired from the navy, and having been one of the search-team leaders who had worked so hard to find *Inchworm*, Senior Chief Haug finally felt compelled to make his feelings known—a full three years after Gerry's remains were found. "Words won't replace the raw emotion I feel when people like [the *Bollard* author] impede success for personal gain," he told me. "The *Bollard* article is a piece that demonstrates artistic freedom from an author who obviously never purposed himself for the betterment of the situation. Instead of grabbing his boots, putting on a pack, and volunteering to look for Gerry, he chose to condemn the very people who did so anonymously." The senior chief's hackles were up.

The anonymity was melting away, and he didn't care. "In our torn, sweat-stained clothing and with bruised and cut bodies, we covered twelve miles the first day, ten miles the next, nine another day, and yet ten more miles another day, in rain and sleet, in some of the toughest terrain in the area. We continued searching through the changing seasons. Miles upon miles, year after year, the search continued so Gerry could go home."

Haug settled down and waxed philosophical:

There's nothing "sinister" about the SERE school or any other training facility in the navy. These are important programs where the main objective is to train our people to have the best chance of survival in some of the most hostile environments on the planet. Those of us who did read the conspiracy theorist's articles were furious, to say the least. Those same sailors, marines, civilians, and contractors the Bollard articles accused are dedicated men and women. We're serving, dammit! We cared about Gerry, and we cared about her family. All the Bollard seemed to do was make up shit . . . How is that helping?

When Haug's search-team member Brett Pehowic first read the articles, he was beside himself.

"Soldiers of fortune?" he said. "We were a good brotherhood . . . a close community. We volunteered with the Boy and Girl Scouts, the Freeport Middle School. We did a lot of good work."

I had dismissed the *Bollard* article once I'd read it, but after interviewing Lieutenant Commander Walker, Dennis Haug, and other SERE personnel and seeing how affected they were by the publication's "scenarios and implications," as Haug referred to them, I researched the pieces more and read a few other articles by the news outlet. They were all agenda-driven pontifications. It's too bad, because the writing is very good.

"How is that helping?" Senior Chief Haug had asked me. There wasn't an easy answer. The authors of the *Bollard* had done their research, and if they had uncovered any piece of evidence that the navy had been involved in some way with Gerry's disappearance, then by all means they should explore that in print. In times of wrongdoing, after all, it is writers and artists who often first take up the fight. From the articles I read by the *Bollard*, I think they fundamentally believe that, too. But there was no evidence to substantiate their damaging innuendo.

One senior Appalachian Trail Conservancy executive I spoke to—who did *not* have the bearing of a military person, by the way—had definite opinions on the *Bollard* articles and the close proximity of the SERE facility to the AT.

"C'mon, man," he said. "That's a group of people who are trained for that sort of stuff. Whatever your feelings about the military are, they really are trained pretty well . . . And actually we're pretty happy to have them there. We've had some potential land-use issues in that area, such as wind power and other development. Having the navy's Redington facility nearby helped stop it. That article was just nonsense."

I found myself leaning on Lieutenant Commander J. D. Walker's dictum: *Logical minds will prevail.*

CHAPTER THIRTEEN

Legacy and Lessons

Now hollow fires burn out to black,
And lights are guttering low:
Square your shoulders, lift your pack,
And leave your friends and go.

Oh never fear, man, nought's to dread,
Look not to left nor right:
In all the endless road you tread
There's nothing but the night.

—A. E. HOUSMAN

Prentiss & Carlisle, a forestry-management company based in central Maine, has been in operation since 1924. In its history, which includes tens of thousands of miles surveying and cruising the North Maine Woods, only once has an employee discovered a body in the woods. It was Gerry.

On the afternoon of October 14, 2015, Lieutenant Kevin Adam was traveling south on Route 15 out of Greenville to check an area for some hunting activity. "I received a call from Scott Stevens on my cell phone," Adam remembers, "which I thought was odd, because I do not hear from him very often." A body had been found up in Redington Township, on the navy property, Stevens told him. Lieutenant Adam felt in his gut it was Gerry. It *had* to be. The hunters would have to wait to have their licenses checked. "I stayed pulled over there on the side of the road for probably thirty minutes, making calls, and then headed towards my house to get ready."

One of the calls he placed was to Joshua Drezek of the Naval Criminal Intelligence Service (NCIS). Kevin Adam very much wanted to know the coordinates of the remains. When he had them, Agent Drezek assured him, he'd forward them to him.

After he had collected his gear, Adam drove to the Comfort Inn in the town of Wilton, Maine. On the way there, the coordinates arrived from Agent Drezek. They were UTM coordinates—Universal Transverse Mercator coordinates. UTM is a global system of grid-based mapping references. Not helpful to Lieutenant Adam while on the road. Adam forwarded them to Game Warden Investigator Joshua Bubier, who was one of the mappers on the service's Incident Management Team, and he converted the UTM coordinates to longitude and latitude, a position format Adam could use. Once he arrived in Wilton, Adam triangulated the position on a map. North of the Appalachian Trail, east of Redington Pond. *That's Gerry*, he thought. *And we were close.*

After two years of thinking about Gerry Largay—of losing sleep over her—Kevin Adam knew there would finally be some closure for himself, for his wardens, for the Appalachian Trail community, and, most important, for her family.

The following day, Lieutenant Adam gathered together some of the game wardens who had been involved in the search for Gerry since the first call for service. Members from the Maine State Police, a group from the state medical examiner's office, federal NCIS officers, a representative from the navy, and a reality TV crew hiked with the surveyor who had found the campsite where Gerry had waited and died. It was a profoundly solemn occasion.

There was her sodden, collapsed tent, right where the surveyors had said it would be. It was most difficult for the wardens. They had spent many hundreds of hours searching for her. They had lost sleep, missed meals, and foregone precious time with loved ones. They had worked themselves sore looking for her. Now they knew where she had been the whole time.

While the state police and the medical examiner's team inspected, cataloged, and cleaned the scene, Lieutenant Adam surveyed his surroundings. He noticed that the tent had been pitched under a hemlock tree, the wide branches above obstructing the view from the sky. He saw that Gerry had taken the time to build up a sort of bedding under her tent, presumably to keep off the moist ground. There was no hearth. Adam looked around some more; there was good firewood and tinder everywhere. While inspecting the site, the wardens found the two small, dead trees that had been scorched by fire. At first glance, the scarring looked like lightning strikes, but a closer inspection revealed they were the work of Gerry. She had tried to signal searchers. "While collecting materials from inside the tent," Lieutenant Adam wrote in his official report, "we came across a small notebook or composition book containing Gerry's writings." Attached was the personal note for her discoverer: *When you find my body, please call my husband George and my daughter Kerry. It will be the greatest kindness to for them to know that I am dead and where you find me—no matter how many years from now. Please find it in your heart to mail the contents of this bag to one of them.*

"Some of the passages inside the book were read," remembers Lieutenant Adam, "and we realized she marked in her book continuous passages up to August 6." As an officer read some of the passages, Lieutenant Adam became uncomfortable; it was obvious there were a lot of personal notes and letters to family members. Kevin Adam had come to know the family. "I asked the officer to stop reading and said we would analyze it all later when we had more time." The rest of the belongings were collected and bagged.

Looking dejected, Adam told the television camera crew from *North Woods Law*, "It's, ah . . . it's heartbreaking." From the footage, it's clear the wardens couldn't care less about the filming. Lieutenant Adam was candid: "She's in a place, just off the trail, that—was—kinda the last place we hadn't got to." As state police photographed the site and the contents of Gerry's tent, the veteran game warden made no excuses. He didn't mention the hundreds of square miles of woods in the area that constitutes "just off the trail." He didn't mention the terrain. Although he'd had many hours to process the moment he found himself in, the sadness was evident in his eyes.

Kris MacCabe, along with Brock Clukey, Patrick Egan, Josh Tibbetts, and other wardens, had been among the first officers to try to find Gerry. MacCabe was also candid. As he faced the reality-television cameras, he was fighting back tears. With stilted speech, he finally spoke: "It's, ah . . . it's hard . . . and, ah, I really . . . I feel for the family." A young warden, who was obviously invested in Gerry's survival, MacCabe struggled to make a statement. "There's—there's nobody else that wanted to bring her home more than we did."

As the state police and the medical examiner's staff bagged up the evidence and carefully prepared to transport Gerry's body, Lieutenant Adam concluded, "We found the body, and we can return her to the family."

Until the state police could process the evidence, and the medical examiner could study the remains, the scene was still a potential crime scene—though unofficially no one expected it actually was. When it was time to go, Lieutenant Adam determined who would carry what off the ridge. He gave the younger wardens the honor of transporting Gerry. They made their way down the ridgeline, through the old cutting, and picked their way along the border of the navy's SERE property and the Appalachian Trail corridor.

Warden Sergeant Scott Thrasher, who had been involved in Gerry's missing-person case from the beginning, spoke to the cameras: "Maine Game Wardens," he said, "including myself . . . we carried her . . . we carried her out. We figured, we were there from the beginning . . . we were gonna . . . we were gonna take her down off that mountain."

Warden Brock Clukey was also asked to speak. "You know," he told the cameras, "it was a real good feeling to . . . you know . . . for the last couple years of being out here searching a real rugged area to . . . bring her home to her family."

More adept at jumping brooks than talking to cameras, the wardens quietly and confidently negotiated the boulders of the stream at the base of the ridge, stepping from rock to rock as they crossed over the water, carrying the evidence bags and the white human-remains pouch. The large, white pouches were stark against the straight, dark spruce forest and the faded hues of orange foliage on the mountainsides.

Once down off the mountain, Warden MacCabe spoke again to the film crew. "This is, ah, something we'll never forget, ah—" MacCabe was trying to hold it together. At one point, trying to stay focused on the words, he appeared to nearly bite his inner cheek. His voice cracking, staring at the forest ground, he said, "Started on this search when it first came out . . . um . . . I know where I was the day I got called, and, ah . . . we all . . . we all wanted to see Gerry come home. And, ah—" He stopped there, still staring at the ground, still clearly wishing with all his heart he had been able to walk Gerry out of those woods two years earlier.

The next morning, while Investigator Bubier attended the autopsy at the Office of the Chief Medical Examiner in Augusta, Lieutenant Kevin Adam was in the same city, holding a press briefing. Two days later, Lieutenant Adam and Warden Investigator Bubier went to the Maine State Police barracks in Gray to pick up Gerry's belongings that had been collected at the campsite. They took several hours to photograph and document the items. There was her green ULA Circuit backpack, her flattened REI-brand tent, and the clothing that had been scattered throughout the tent. There was her little yellow whistle and the tiny compass on a keychain. There were Ziploc bags—many of them. One of the baggies held the notebook with the annotation "George Please Read XOXO."

There was a clear sack with candles and matches in a waterproof container. Another bag contained a small first-aid kit, lighters, and sewing materials. There was a tattered Mylar space blanket. In one bag was a tiny homemade necklace with a small white stone, wrapped in string.

Her cell phone was there, and it would be dropped off at Maine's Computer Crimes lab. A report generated from the lab showed the same calls that the 2013 exigent warrant from Verizon had revealed. The last text was the one she'd sent George on August 6, which of course he'd never received. She had taken no videos or photographs.

In one of the evidence bags was the small bottle of body powder that she and Terry Bliss had joked about two years earlier at Eliza Brook Shelter. Another bag enclosed papers headed "Follow Terry's Hike," printed from his blog, TerryBliss.com.

The wardens also recovered a moldy, moss-covered paperback, with some of the pages removed. In one baggie was a folded sheet of paper with the prayers of the rosary.

On October 23, forensic DNA analysis confirmed that the person from the campsite was Geraldine Largay. The medical examiner's report would reveal there were no signs of trauma. It would list the cause of death as inanition—death from exposure and failure to thrive. She had starved.

When the time came, Gerry's was a dignified homecoming, her faith firmly intact. She was carried out of the mountains with dignity and respect. Her family could lay her to rest. In her journal were letters to loved ones. They are private letters and will be cherished by her descendants. Her determination and fortitude emanates through her writing.

Two weeks after the DNA results were completed, Lieutenant Adam, Gerry's family, and a few wardens visited her final campsite. There her family left a cross along with some mementoes. On the cross were some inscriptions. One from a grandchild, in youthful script, reads simply "I wish you were here."

Two years earlier, on October 12, 2013, George had a memorial service for Gerry at Saint Brigid Catholic Church in Johns Creek, Georgia. A notification for those interested had been posted on Facebook. A table had been set up in the reception hall with mementoes of Gerry that the congregants had brought—a hiking boot, one of Gerry's quilts, some photographs, and other mementos. Jane Lee brought along a white alabaster rock that she carried. (She and Gerry had occasionally picked up interesting little rocks along the way, placing them on the cairns that often mark the trail. A few stones they kept.) Jane had held on to one pretty, white stone. "Gerry used to call it 'our Saint Alabaster—our hiking saint,'" she remembers. "So many people whose lives Gerry touched were represented on the table—quilters, birders, hikers, and friends."

Tim *Walker* McElhannon was there, and he was able to meet Gerry's children but was only able to speak to George briefly. Kit Parks was there as well. "The memorial was amazing," she said. "I was touched that she had been keeping up with friends she'd had for more than forty years. Friends from all facets of her life attended. People flew in from everywhere. The church was packed."

Gerry's son-in-law tried to say a few words about Gerry but could not get through it; George had to finish for him.

On the Appalachian Trail, Gerry had befriended people, and her loss touched many. Her story has changed how her trail acquaintances hike and behave—even how they think.

Even now, Betty Anne Schenk, Gerry's oldest friend, still thinks of her childhood companion constantly. Going back all the way to Girl Scout Troop 433 in Tampa in the 1960s, "BA" and Gerry's bond was unbreakable. Separate from the Largay's hiking-community friends, Betty Anne, Gerry, and George were in a circle of friends who met as often as possible and traveled internationally together, which of course tightens the bonds of friendship.

"I'm not sure how to tell you about the bonding between Gerry's friends since we lost her," Betty Anne told me. "In April 2016, we gathered to make a garden for Gerry at the trailhead of the 'Largay Link' in the network of trails on our property in North Carolina—a trail Gerry helped us build. Gerry's sister was there. Each of us brought plants to contribute and a little memorial item. Then we shared some wine and told Gerry stories. We laugh at the things she did. We e-mail still and talk. It seems to help to share her memory."

Betty Anne became reminiscent: "Growing up, Gerry was always positive. She was always smart and interested in learning—anything. Best of all was her sense of humor, which never quit." There was a pause. I waited for it. "She was outgoing and personable. She was *fun*."

Jane Lee's life changed because of Gerry. Jane felt anguish at her friend's passing. For a long time, she replayed different scenarios in her head. She had gone looking for her friend several times, at least once by herself. Jane still hikes when she can and thinks of *Inchworm* every time. "I had never been on a long hike without her," Jane said in 2017. "It has gotten easier, but I still feel like my other hiking half is missing. At times, I do feel her presence with me on the trails. I think of her every day—not really in sadness but how I should strive to be as kind and generous as her."

Jane still carries her little "Saint Alabaster" rock. For luck, yes, but it's also a little part of her friend, still going up and down the trails, one inch at a time.

Tim McElhannon finished his thru-hike on August 4, 2013, while Gerry was still alive. The following year, he and his wife hiked the Portuguese route of the Camino de Santiago. In 2015, he hiked for eight days on the Long Trail in Vermont and then spent some of the summer doing volunteer trail work for the Appalachian Trail Conservancy.

Also in 2015, Tim saw an article marking the two-year anniversary of Gerry's disappearance. After two years of living with a nagging discomfort, Tim and his wife decided it was time to call Lieutenant Kevin Adam. Tim was the hiker who had spent the most time with Gerry and George in those last days before she got lost, and he could not shake the odd feeling he'd gotten from his last encounter with them on the hike into Poplar Ridge. With the facts known, it is easy to dismiss the couple's change in affect when Tim spoke with them; it's possible that George was trying to convince *Inchworm* to quit her trek, realizing it was getting too difficult for her. It matters no longer. But for two years, Tim had wrestled with the knowledge that George was a good man—and that he very much liked him—and with his sense of civic duty to report any small bit of information to the wardens. For well over a year, Tim couldn't shake the nagging feeling. He finally made the call.

Tim reported to Lieutenant Adam what he had experienced the last time he saw Gerry and George on the trail, the day before she disappeared. Kevin Adam spoke with Tim for quite a while. "Based on my experience," said Lieutenant Adam, "Gerry's body will be found one day." Furthermore, Adam told Tim that he'd seen people deal with grief in very different ways and that he was not suspicious of George. That sealed it for Tim; he felt enormous relief. He had never really thought George could've been involved in his wife's disappearance, but it felt good to have any niggling suspicions allayed. Three years after his call to Lieutenant Adam, Tim is still embarrassed about the misgivings he once harbored, and he might never have mentioned it at all except that it offers "a great lesson in not relying too much on your instinct in these matters, especially when you don't have much experience in such matters."

Lieutenant Adam had been prophetic in their conversation: Gerry's body would be found a couple of months later.

In 2016, Tim made the trip to Nepal, where he hiked to Everest Base Camp and climbed Gokyo Ri and Kala Patthar. "The elevation made it very challenging, but the terrain was not as tough as the AT is in Maine and New Hampshire." He no longer lives in Virginia. He still hikes whenever he can, and he often thinks of Gerry and George and their time together. "I was very fond of them both," said Tim. "Hopefully Gerry can continue to inspire others to hike the trail—perhaps with some self-rescue training. She'd like that, I think—helping others, even after she's gone."

Dianne *Gummy Bear* Cook, the Canadian woman who had hiked with Gerry in early July, remembers her fondly.

"During the time that I was hiking with her," said Dianne in 2018, "she seemed to only eat mint Oreo cookies, and she was really skinny, though I didn't eat any meals with her—only stopped for snacks with her."

"George doesn't like mint," Gerry had told Dianne. "So I know I'll have a stash of cookies."

"During the time when we were hiking together," remembers Dianne, "Gerry was day hiking, and then George would pick her up, and they would eat in town. She was slow, but no slower that other women that I met her age on the trail. I had to slow down a lot the two days I was on the trail with her."

"I still think of her," said Dianne. "I'm amazed that Gerry lived so long in the woods with no food. I really regret not joining the search afterwards knowing that she was alive for a month afterwards. I think it's a testament to her survival skills and knowledge as a nurse. The one sad thing is that I know that she had a GPS SPOT device but hadn't figured out how to use it. It was in the SUV. I offered to help them set it up, but Gerry said that she was okay without it."

Dianne also worries about George's well-being. "The two of them really seemed like amazing life partners. When we were hiking, Gerry would talk about him." *Inchworm* had said, "I was really lucky to have married him."

For David Field, who for decades had tended the very section of trail where Gerry got lost and knew it and its corridors intimately, not being asked to advise the search efforts was a sore spot for some time.

In January 2014, Lieutenant Adam had met with the Maine Appalachian Trail Club to talk about ways to improve future searches along the trail. Minutes of the meeting follow:

> *At the time of that search, the Warden Service tried to make contact with MATC, knowing that maintainers would have detailed information and knowledge of the Trail and access points. Unfortunately, communications broke down, and some opportunities were missed. At least two District Overseers did try to make contact to give information, but their messages didn't reach the proper authorities. Members of the MATC Executive Committee reported that there was a protocol in years past, but, as personnel changed, information regarding those procedures was lost. Dave Field noted that the Local Management Plan does list all contact information, but it needs to be updated. In conclusion, members of the MATC Executive Committee and Lt. Adam urged that both entities reestablish links between local rescue operations and MATC District Overseers. Claire Polfus offered that she can serve as resource as she's on the trail a lot and talks with hikers. She also urged that information on contact procedure should be written, both at the local level and with ATC, and should be updated on a regular basis. Kevin asked that MATC designate one or two people to serve as contact with wardens and searchers.*

Later that year, David had guided some members of the Appalachian Long Distance Hikers Association up the lower slopes of Poplar Ridge. Standing in a wide spot on Railroad Road, appearing remarkably fit for his age and looking every bit the professional forester, David had faced the group and addressed some of the theories that were abounding at the time in the media.

Ticking off points on his left hand, one finger at a time, he reviewed the conjecturing: "'It's the husband, it's always the husband.' Well, you look at the history of this, and that's ridiculous." Next finger: "'Some rogue from the navy survival training camp'"—here David pointed up Railroad Road—"'grabbed her and hauled her off.' Well, no." Another finger: "'She walked out this road, and she's on a beach in Rio now.' No. For her to get out of here without being seen, in fact, there were so many hikers and volunteers along the trail looking for her, for her to slip out unseen between hikers would've been impossible."

"My theory," David had said, "and it's simply logic, is that she had a stroke or suffered a concussion or *something* that impaired her mentally but not physically, so she was able to crash off through the underbrush so far that the dogs couldn't smell her. I can't think of any other thing that makes sense—and once you get out that far, I got to tell you, this country, I'm a professional forester . . . I've gone through these woods with map and compass and wouldn't hesitate to go anywhere. But if you don't have that background and equipment, you can get into trouble in a hell of a hurry." It hadn't occurred to David at that time that it might not have been mental impairment, but rather a reliance on cell phone technology, that had driven Gerry to "crash off through the underbrush."

Kit Parks has also been hard hit by Gerry's passing. She hikes a lot every year all over the world and never fails to think of Gerry. "I'm so glad she was in the class I took with Warren Doyle at the Appalachian Trail Institute," she told me in 2017. "It was more fun because she and George were there." As she recalls,

Gerry was very knowledgeable about flora and fauna and often pointed out some of her favorites. I remember her teaching me about the big, leafy plant galax that grows in the Appalachians and her thrill at discovering a cluster of lady's slippers. She showed me where wild boars were rooting up the soil in search of a meal. Along the trail, we often came across these clusters of hundreds of mini, bright-orange toadstools. We nicknamed them "villages" and were always delighted when we saw a new bunch on a rotted fallen tree. We saw dozens upon dozens of these villages. I have yet to see that kind of mushroom since. On the last day of our section hike, I was hiking ahead and met a mushroom scientist. I asked him about the villages. He wasn't sure what I was talking about, which I thought strange. I also told him about a "five-star fungi" I'd seen on a tree near Jones Falls, so he immediately set out to see this specimen. Memories like those—that's pure Gerry.

Kit talked to me about my writing this book: "Perhaps we hikers get complacent and think that well-marked trails such as the AT don't require any backwoods skill. I hope your book does indeed help us non-regular 'backwooders' realize that life isn't Disneyland and sometimes things don't go as planned so we need to be prepared."

"One other thing," Kit remembered. "The summer after we lost her, I was on a camping/biking trip in Damascus, Virginia, where I first met Gerry. It was on an afternoon to hike on the AT where we first bonded and she gave me a space blanket. When I returned to my car and started to back up the car and had my hands on the steering wheel, I noticed on my left hand a small green inchworm. I hadn't seen an inchworm in years. I put 'Gerry' back in the woods and drove off. I don't know . . . I just think of her a lot."

Dottie *.Com* Rust and Regina *Queen* Clark, both from Maryland, have been extremely affected by Gerry's passing. Their time they spent with her at Poplar Ridge the morning she went missing has left no small impression. Not only do they think of her often, but they've also changed the way they hike. And since both women hike so regularly, it's as though they've changed their culture—or lifestyle.

Regina still works as a registered nurse and thinks of *Inchworm* a great deal of the time: "I continue to hike and hold Gerry close each day I spend on the trail. I would like her family to know she lives on through her 'trail family.' I think of all the people she met and all the lives she touched. Quite amazing, really. And I know my family thinks of her each time I pack for a hiking trip."

During the two years before Gerry's remains were found, Dottie continued her section hikes to complete the AT. "I often section hiked solo," she remembers, "and it would be during those nights especially that I would wonder about *Inchworm*. I would set up my small tent for the night, crawl in, write in my journal, and finally set things aside to find sleep. I would gaze out of the tent into the black night and wonder, *Whatever happened to you, Gerry? Where are you?*"

"After her remains were found," Dottie recalled in 2016, "and her last journal entries were made public, my thoughts turned to *How did you endure so many days and nights as you did? Were you very scared? I'm so sorry this happened to you.* And, of course, I thought about her family as well."

"Just those twelve hours with *Inchworm* marked me and changed me for life," says Dottie. "My quest to finish the Appalachian Trail—and I'm sure I would have anyway—but what I took away from meeting Gerry was an inspiration, with a new, real feeling of being empowered, and I knew I would finish my quest."

According to Dottie,

The Appalachian Trail in the South is not nearly as thick as it is in Maine. And in the Southern states, I always felt I could "see" the trail . . . It is always nearby. Never had I paid attention to how far I walked off the trail. Gerry's story has changed my hiking habits. What happened to Inchworm could happen to me—or to any other hiker, really. Now when I need to relieve myself, I find a place closer to the trail, and I don't care if someone might see me . . . I tell them, "Avert your eyes, please!" I also leave a hiking pole stuck in the ground on the side of the trail, and I turn and keep that pole in sight. Because of Gerry, I would not leave the trail in the North Maine Woods. Period.

Sitting on boulders next to the Appalachian Trail in Harpers Ferry, Dottie and I conversed about her time with Gerry. Hikers strode by as we talked. In the middle of our interview, while discussing how easy it is to get turned around on the AT, a middle-aged man stopped dead in his tracks when he got to us. "Is this the AT?" he wanted to know. "Yes, it is," said Dottie. "Am I headed south or north?" Dottie gave the man all the information he needed to know, and after he left, we just looked at each other.

In July 2017, my friend and assistant Doug Comstock and I hiked in to "Gerry's site" with Dottie and her husband, Mark. There was apprehension in Dottie's eyes as we hiked up Railroad Road and along the Appalachian Trail. She seemed to be hiking much more slowly than she had the summer before when we'd taken a walk on the AT in Harpers Ferry. Today there was purpose in her steps. We took a compass bearing from the AT and bushwhacked through the old cuttings, deadfalls, and witch hobble. We were quiet as we forded the same two streams that Gerry had four years earlier. As we climbed up the steep ridge to *Inchworm*'s campsite, Doug and I skirted around to the side at the summit. With her memorial cross in sight, we stopped and gestured for them to walk past us. Dottie, not one to wear her emotions on her sleeve, took two more steps and stopped. Staring through the trees at the cross placed at Gerry's tent site, she burst into tears. It seemed to take her by surprise.

Mark walked to the cross with his wife and then held back by a few steps when they got to it. He wanted her to have a moment with Gerry. Dottie knelt by the cross and wept. I fought back tears as Mark stepped forward to put a hand on Dottie's back and they mourned together. Doug and I turned and walked farther away to give them privacy. After some time, we rejoined them and paid our respects, and then the four of us talked about the search. From high on that ridge, I could point out where the K-9s had been and where the wardens, volunteers, and navy DBAP searchers had come through. None had been close enough to find her. "I can't believe how remote this feels," said Dottie.

Dottie removed from her pack a small print, wrapped in plastic, of the now-famous photo she'd taken of Gerry at Poplar Ridge and leaned it against the cross where she had died. That image meant a lot to Dottie. Sometimes there is a special glow in a moment, and often that moment is realized in retrospect. In the words passed between them that night in the Poplar Ridge shelter was an inspiration that will last a lifetime. When Dottie had taken that photo, she could not have known that it would change her life.

Our thoughts belonged to Gerry and her family. Dottie clearly cared about *Inchworm*. "Twelve hours," she said, still crying. "Half a day with someone can have such an effect on you. Truly amazing."

I first met retired Senior Chief Dennis Haug in 2017 in a restaurant outside of Portland, Maine. Our meeting had been set up by Lieutenant Commander J. D. Walker. My twenty-one-year-old son accompanied me to the meeting with a view to going fishing afterward. My back was toward the restaurant entrance (a bold strategy when meeting someone for the first time). My son suddenly looked up from his salad toward the entrance. "This is him."

"How do you know?" I asked.

"Yeah . . . he's military," said my boy.

I liked Dennis right away. For an obviously tough, capable, and confident young man, talking about the search for Gerry clearly put him on edge. I had read the *Bollard* article by then, and as I conducted my own research, I was still trying to figure out how the navy had been involved with the search, if at all. I didn't mention the articles at the beginning of the meeting. I simply asked him whether he had looked for Gerry.

"Going over the maps," I told him, "it looks to me like a couple of teams got really close to her."

"I think we did," he said. "Maybe a hundred yards." I was silent. I wasn't sure whether he was finished talking as he studied my map. "It still stings a bit."

Dennis sat back in his chair and let it all go. He told us how his DBAP search-and-rescue people had been put on standby on Wednesday night and then were called to join the search late Thursday night. He was in New Hampshire, so, after organizing his gear and saying goodbye to his family, he drove through the night to meet the search party by Friday morning. He talked about the terrain. He talked about the pain of not finding her and how the pain was still very much a part of his life.

We looked again at the spot marked in pencil on my map. "This is where Gerry died," I said. The spot was from my calculations, where I had triangulated the coordinates. He cocked his head to the side as he studied it. "Looks right," he said. "Pretty close to the navy property." (The media were all saying Gerry had passed away on the SERE land.)

"Have you been in?" he asked. I nodded.

Dennis could obviously walk in there on his own easily. I asked him whether he had been to the site. He sat back in his chair and squared his sizeable shoulders.

"I can't," he said. "Not yet. I don't think I'm ready." I was surprised by his response.

"Understand," he said, "this was a difficult deal for us. We don't like to leave anyone behind, whether it's a Marine in the Sandbox or a sixty-six-year-old woman on the Appalachian Trail." I nodded again.

"Personally," Dennis confided, "I've been affected a lot by this over the past two years. I've lost sleep over her."

I went out on a limb. After an awkward pause, I asked if, because of my connection to Gerry's story, he would like to accompany my research assistant and me to the site.

"No, thank you." His reply was quick. "I'm just not ready."

"Okay," I said. "If you ever change your mind, please let me know. I realize you don't need me to show you the way" (I smiled), "but it'd be an honor."

Dennis smiled back but didn't say anything else about it.

A week later, Senior Chief Haug called me. "I've thought it over," he said. "I think I'd like to go to the site. Might be good for me."

So that August, Doug Comstock and I met Dennis in Phillips, Maine. He followed us to the tiny hamlet of East Madrid, about six miles down in the valley below Gerry's campsite. We drove as far as we could up Railroad Road, to the same spot we'd been with Dottie and Mark Rust the summer before. We then walked up the road a mile to where it crosses the Appalachian Trail.

Dennis did not hike slowly. He was machinelike in his manner on the trail. He was hard to keep up with. Doug kept pace, no problem. The same age as me—late fifties—Doug has kept in great shape by, of course, hiking. I just toddled up behind them whenever I got the chance. When we took a compass bearing and started bushwhacking toward Gerry's site, Dennis slowed his pace. We were cutting through the Appalachian Trail corridor. As we neared the navy's SERE property, he started teaching. He couldn't help it . . . he was in his element. He started talking about the feast around us and would bend over, pluck a plant, tell us about it, and then matter-of-factly eat it.

"You can make quite a salad in the summertime in these woods," he said. "Every day."

The first plant he came across was about fifty yards from the AT. "This is trillium," he told us. "You have to boil the leaves. In early spring, its taste is cucumberlike. However, once the flower appears, in July or August, when Gerry was here, it has quite a bitter taste. But it's nourishment. Try to eat it only in an emergency. It's a protected plant in some places."

Dennis took about thirty more steps. "This is great," he said, bending over with his forty-five-pound pack. "This one's wood sorrel." The little plant had cloverlike heart-shaped leaves, and there was a lot of it. "This can be eaten straight from the ground," he explained, munching on a handful. "You can collect it and make a huge salad. You can eat the leaves and the stems. It tastes a little like apples . . . sour apples. It's great because it's high in vitamin C."

We all ate some, and I liked the wood sorrel.

Another hundred paces, and we clambered up and over some old slash left piled up from a woodcutting operation, probably in the 1950s, and then half walked, half slid down next to the bank of the first of the two brooks we would have to cross. Near the brook, Dennis stopped again. He felt the tops of some ostrich ferns with the palm of his hand.

"These are good also," he said. Dennis knew Doug and I had both grown up in Maine, so it was likely that we had eaten fiddleheads every spring almost as a ritual. "You guys probably like fiddleheads." (Fiddleheads picked in early spring before the ferns unfurl are boiled and then cooked in butter and taste, to some, like asparagus—only better.) "But you know you can eat them in summer, too. If you dig up the root ball and separate them, you'll find the little curled shoots that'll pop up the following spring. You still must boil them. They'll keep you alive, but you wouldn't want to eat them for much more than a month or two. Some people think that could have some negative health effects." He didn't say what they were, but we believed him.

We crossed the brook and climbed another couple of ridges, taking us farther away from the AT. Every time I've hiked to the site, I've gotten scrapes and cuts on my legs and arms from the slash and the "pucker-brush." This trip was no different.

We were not using GPS. Dennis, Doug, and I are coincidentally of the same mind regarding GPS technology: it's great, but there's no substitute for a map and compass (and knowing how to use them) when it comes to the backcountry. We moved along our compass bearing, and halfway up a steep ridge I recognized a particular tree. It was Gerry's ridge. I looked over at Doug, who was the pathfinder that day, and he nodded. As with Dottie and Mark Rust the summer before, Doug and I slowed down so Dennis could have a moment alone. We knew by then that the pain he felt for not having found *Inchworm* was real.

"She was up there," I said to Dennis. He didn't look up the hill. He immediately looked around him at the terrain—up the drainage we had just traversed, back at the last brook we'd crossed. After pondering his surroundings, something inside him clicked, and he resolutely climbed to the top of the ridge. I was amazed that once he'd reconnoitered, he knew exactly where he was. He quickly forged ahead of us. We followed him to the top of the ridge.

There was no poking around or looking for a campsite or a cross; as Doug and I crested the hill, he had already found it. There was Dennis, leaning on his trekking poles, solemnly quiet, head down, paying his respects at Gerry's tent site. We gave him some time. We could see he was upset—not tearful, but something different. He was sad, certainly, but it was almost as if he were pissed off. He took her loss personally.

After a few moments, he dropped his pack and started pulling things from it. By the time Doug and I walked up to the site, Dennis had his compass out, along with maps, printouts of GPS tracks, a pencil, and notes. He drew lines on the map. He did some math.

"That's the trouble with different search groups using different types of maps," Dennis said to us. "We weren't a hundred to two hundred meters from her. It was more like six hundred meters." While the maps the navy DBAP searchers had used were marked with both longitude and latitude and the UTM coordinates, the wardens will often print out maps for their search teams from Topo, Garmin, or DeLorme map sources. The Warden Service relies heavily on Garmin GPS for tracking. It's the only effective way to be certain they've cleared each search area. They record each GPS-generated track route from each team and color-code them. For instance, a K-9 unit's track logs are red. It did not change anything for Dennis, finding out that he had not been as close to Gerry as he had thought. For him, he had been close enough. He, his team, and the wardens are still haunted by the fact that Gerry died alone on the hilltop.

At the site, some things made no sense. Why was there no hearth? Why was she camped under the canopy of a hemlock tree when fifty yards away the forest was much clearer to the sky?

I noticed close at hand some of that edible sorrel Dennis had shown us and, at arm's length, the fire-starting material. "There's plenty of stuff to eat around here, if you know what you're doing," said Dennis. He started talking about teaching people survival skills and how much he has enjoyed "giving people that edge" over the years. In that moment, his long-held idea for a survival school became a conviction.

We talked a bit about Gerry's circuitous route between where she likely had left the Appalachian Trail and her final campsite. We marveled at how tough she was. A quick glance at our compass showed us where north was, and we knew if we turned our bodies 160 degrees to the right, we would be heading south-southeast—directly toward Railroad Road, where wardens, K-9 teams, and volunteers had been shuttling back and forth for two weeks looking for her.

We looked at the brook (Gerry's water supply and where she had washed her clothes) at the bottom of the hill. None of us could understand her decision to not follow that brook downstream, as we three had been taught as youngsters. Perhaps that's the thing: we were *taught* what to do if lost in the woods. We agreed that it was likely she had misjudged how quickly the debilitation of her health would descend upon her—that she had probably entertained the idea but had become too weak too quickly to aid in her self-rescue.

After offering a prayer and paying our respects to Gerry, we made a decision: we would walk down to the brook and follow it down. Would doing so have helped Gerry? All three of us were sure it would have.

Standing at the edge of the water, I said, "Let's suppose we're a sixty-six-year-old woman who is tired, a little beat-up, and we haven't consumed any calories in a week. We're in a deconditioned state and extremely weak. So let's take our time see where we end up. If it gets too late, we'll take a compass bearing for the AT."

So we did. We picked our way along the rocks and sticks along the bank of the brook, following the gurgling water as it tumbled between two ridges. The boulders in the brook were all carpeted with bright, emerald-green moss, wet with spray. The going was very difficult. The other side of the brook looked, as it always does, to be gentler walking, so we crossed over. Slowly, carefully, as the weak, older, extremely stressed "hiker" that we were pretending to be, we picked our way across the slippery rocks. It was easier walking on the far side. In fact, a very old tote road followed the brook down on that side. It was overgrown with spruce, fir, and small birch trees, so it was still arduous, but we labored through it.

Ever on the lookout for things to eat, Dennis knelt at a spot where the softwood trees gave way to some more sparsely spaced hardwoods on the slope of a smaller ridge.

"Bunchberry," he said. "This low-to-the-ground-growing plant has berries during the late summer that are really pretty good to eat. They don't have any taste, but they have vitamins." The berries were in a cluster. "When you pick the cluster, they fall apart into single berries. They would have been all over here when Gerry was camped. You can't just eat berries randomly, or you'll find yourself getting really sick. And that's the thing with berries: you have to *know* which ones are okay."

Even taking our time, even stopping for a lesson on the value of bunchberries, and even though we were slowed down by my falling into the brook as we forded it, forty-three minutes after leaving Gerry's tent site we popped out onto Railroad Road, 2,100 feet west of where the Appalachian Trail crosses it. If we walked east, we were a two-minute walk from the boundary of the navy SERE property. It might have been the saddest moment of our trip. We all knew that Railroad Road had been bustling with searchers, especially in the first five days of the search. On several search days, where we stood was where the dogs had been cast with the K-9 teams.

We walked down the old railroad bed to the AT crossing. We decided that would be a good place to camp for the night—to decompress and to discuss Dennis's experience during the search for Gerry. Without saying a word, we spread out along the grass and gravel tote road about fifty feet apart and set up our bivouac sites. In ten minutes, we were all finished. We converged next to Doug's tent, not far from the AT, where it emerges from the steep climb up from Orbeton Stream.

"Fire?" asked Doug. Dennis and I nodded. After a quick construction of a ring and a small collection of firewood, Dennis reached into the bushes from the edge of the road. He knew what he was looking for. In seconds, he had a tiny bundle of tinder from two or three sources. He took a few steps to a small balsam tree, snapped a twig from a branch, and popped a blister on its bark. He rubbed one side of the tinder into the sap that oozed from the blister. Watching him brought back fond memories of my father. Dennis matter-of-factly walked up to the tiny pile of twigs and shoved the tinder (sappy end first) into the twigs. He pulled a piece of flint and a striker from his pocket and aimed the device at the tinder, and with one whack sparks flew, and the fire started. Nothing to it. He fed the twigs with progressively larger sticks and pieces of dried bark, and we staked out our places to sit around the little fire.

"When I was in SAR," I said, staring into the fire, "I had noticed that most of the upper-level searchers were all type A personalities—competitive, confident, highly organized, ambitious. That personality type includes the wardens, for the most part."

"Still are," said Dennis, smiling.

When working together, the type A's can clash occasionally. When Dennis and his team had shown up on the first Friday of Gerry's search early in the morning at the mobile incident command vehicle on Sugarloaf Mountain, one of the wardens who realized the DBAP searchers had been up most of the previous night postured and said directly to Dennis, "You're the guy I'm going to have to pull off the trail at nine o'clock this morning." Dennis, who is an absolute animal on the trails and in the woods, even with a heavy pack, said nothing. One of his team members just laughed and said, "Man, you don't know him."

"Every one of them wants to be the person who walks out of the woods with the lost soul. Or carry them out," I mused.

"They wouldn't be out there beating themselves up if they didn't," Dennis said. "But it always comes back to wanting to help people. A lot of searchers, especially the volunteers, are in the medical field, or they're volunteer firemen in their communities or ambulance drivers. For the DBAP team, we're military or ex-military; we all consider our service—in our case, the navy—as fundamentally helping people." Then Dennis sat back on his rock and straightened his back. "That's why some of the stuff we read stung so much."

I changed the subject temporarily. "There were so many theories as to what happened to Gerry—falling out of sight into a crevice, leaving the trail on her own for wanting to start a new life, abduction . . . murder. Even uxoricide." No one spoke.

"Did you know that the wardens received a letter suggesting Bigfoot took her?" I asked. Doug, who is very quick with a joke, looked at me over the fire but held it in check. I thought he might have a seizure. He has a lot of Bigfoot jokes. It wasn't the time.

"I remember at the time the search was going on," I said, "the investigators pretty easily ruled out all but two possible scenarios: that she did indeed fall into a crevice, out of sight, between two huge granite slabs and died either from the fall or from thirst, or that she simply wandered throughout the forests and dug herself into some remote, difficult spot, which of course we know now was accurate."

"This technology—it can be a problem," said Doug. "She worked so hard to find cell service, and, not finding it, she had to fall back on survival skills. Which we know weren't there. It's heart-wrenching." Doug looked frustrated. "If she'd just followed one of the friggin' brooks, she'd have walked right to here." Doug pointed at his feet. "Or to the navy property. Either direction, she'd have been found."

Dennis was doing some math in his head. "What?" I asked. He took a moment to finish his calculations and then spoke.

"*If* she had followed the first brook she came to downstream," he said, "and *if* she had turned in this direction when she hit the Railroad Road, traveling, say, one-half mile per hour because she'd have been bushwhacking . . ."—Dennis looked up at the nearby Appalachian Trail sign where the trail enters the woods northbound: "SPAULDING MOUNTAIN . . . 6.1 miles"—"she probably would've only lost five hours on her hike to Spaulding. If she followed the second brook, six hours— she could have camped right here" (besides us, there were already three other AT hikers "stealth" camping nearby) "and she would have met her husband a day late, with a good story to tell."

I listened while Dennis and Doug talked for some time about the fact that knowing how to use a compass is a more important tool than knowing what type of water filter to buy or what brand of backpack— which hikers will agonize over for weeks before pulling the trigger—yet many give no thought to learning map and compass. Some don't even take one on the trail, which we found ridiculous. Gerry's compass, we noted, was too small to navigate with—not in a life-and-death situation. At her campsite, she had practiced using her tiny button compass in line-of-site trials by walking from one tree to another, but surely she was frustrated with its limitations. (As a study, I purchased a similar tiny compass and tried to use it. Whenever I found "north," I could twist my wrist or turn my torso and the needle pointing north would change completely—sometimes 180 degrees from its original orientation.)

In 2015, at the time of year when thru-hikers would be finishing the Hundred-Mile Wilderness, I'd sat with a trail-magic guy near Abol Campground, where the Appalachian Trail pops out onto Golden Road, west of the town of Millinocket. Situated along the south entrance to Baxter State Park, Abol famously marks the "homestretch" for northbound AT thru-hikers. As the trail angel passed out sodas, lemonade, candy, and snacks to hungry, bug-bitten hikers, I had asked each of them two questions: "Do you know how to use a compass?" and "Did you carry one?"

In the two days I sat there (with intermittent trips down the banks of the West Branch of the Penobscot to fly fish), I had posed the questions to twenty-one thru-hikers.

- Three had confidently said yes to both questions, and all three said they never go into the woods without a compass.

- Two (a couple) had said they carried one but weren't sure they could actually use it correctly.

- One had said he hadn't brought one but wished he had, mentioning that he had found himself turned around twice in the Hundred-Mile Wilderness.

- *Fifteen*, unbelievably, had said no to both questions. A few pointed out that "a compass isn't necessary for hiking trails like the AT," to which I had said, cheerfully, "Okay, thanks!" and made my entry in my notebook.

Then I had followed up with "Did you happen to stay or stop at the Poplar Ridge shelter on the way up?" (Most of them had.) "Cool. Was the memorial to Gerry Largay still there?"

More than 71 percent of the hikers I questioned in two days had given no apparent thought to the importance of a compass or what to do if lost in a forest.

Now, a year later, staring into the flames of the campfire, listening to Dennis and Doug come up with a few rather brilliant ideas for self-rescue and discussing the pitfalls of relying on cell phone technology, I remembered something a friend had e-mailed to me recently. He had come across an article from Verizon Wireless about a drone being used by that company as a "flying cell site," to potentially offer cell coverage in what the industry calls "coverage-denied environments," like the one where Gerry had been. The technology has been developed by a team at Verizon and American Aerospace Technologies, Inc., led by principal engineer Christopher Desmond, out of Houston. The technology was developed originally for disaster scenarios, such as hurricanes. My friend, a remarkably compassionate man, knew about the book I was writing and had followed Gerry's story. In his e-mail, he told me he hoped that as drone technology and advances become readily available, perhaps they will be used for mountain rescues.

There are some kinks to work out, like the availability of the drones and the fact that small "chase planes" must fly with the drones, a requirement when flying the drone beyond visual line of sight. Obviously the weather would have to cooperate. Then there's the lost person on the ground: they would need to have a spare battery or a battery charger that can charge the battery up to five times.

Advancing communication capabilities is an excellent idea, and I'm no Luddite, but there in the woods—the same woods Gerry had walked through—I kept finding myself going back to basics. What if you lose your charger in some bushes or fall into the brook like I had or smashed your phone on a rock? If the "flying cell sites" save one person in the future because everything lines up for the lost person (good phone, good charger, good weather), then that'll be wonderful. Verizon should be excited about the prospect—a lot of people have worked very hard to bring it to fruition. However, from a hiking point of view, it is very concerning. Hikers, hunters, anglers, and other outdoor enthusiasts becoming ever more reliant on technology that may or may not be available is not the answer.

As I opened my journal, unsure what to write, I wanted to broach the topic with Dennis and Doug.

I asked their opinions. Dennis spoke first. "What? Instead of teaching each other how to help ourselves if we become lost—how to build a shelter or a fire, to use a compass, or to know when to stay put or when to follow a stream—instead, we'll just 'Dial a Rescue'?"

Doug said, "I think it's important that people learn what to do. If that means reading books or taking a course, then do it. I've seen how amazing a compass can be. You can walk a straight line through the woods for a mile with a compass bearing." Then he said, "Of course, it helps if you know which direction you *want* to go."

We all agreed: The less reliance on technology in the woods, the better. Period. The more educated we can become about what to do if lost, the better. It sounds so simple; yet vast numbers of people think navigation competence unnecessary.

Given that Gerry had not acquired the necessary skills to surviving in the backcountry, one cannot help but lament the GPS SPOT locator that had purposefully been left in the Toyota Highlander. This is just like the maps and compasses that Brian King at the Appalachian Trail Conservancy had told me are too frequently left behind; the culture of the trail says they're not needed. They are extra weight—if only a few ounces.

Doug, Dennis, and I talked about her search. Everybody wanted a clean story, I said. People wanted to know what happened, or they wanted to blame someone or something. The problem with that is that no one looking for her was to blame—certainly not the wardens, whose efforts were herculean. (There is just too much wilderness real estate where Gerry was. It would have been impossible to cover every inch of it in two weeks, even with five hundred volunteers.) It wasn't George's fault. It wasn't the volunteers'. Even the bits of misinformation given to the wardens that shifted resources weren't to blame. And it wasn't the navy's, God knows.

I even think that beyond the personal responsibility to learn self-rescue techniques, it wasn't Gerry's fault, either. It was simply tragic. Given her age, the increasing difficulty of the trail, and her lack of woodscraft, the shift from safety to danger was not improbable. It was a tragedy that could've been avoided. She just hadn't prepared for what to do if she got lost, and she's not alone in that among hikers on the AT.

Dennis agreed. "Well, it's every individual's responsibility to learn what they can. But, really, Mrs. Largay was no exception; hardly anyone who thru-hikes the Appalachian Trail learns survival skills, as far as I can tell. I hope I'm wrong."

"At one point," I said, "George told the wardens that perhaps she was in over her head."

"But not on the trail," said Doug. "She had just knocked off nine hundred miles."

"That's true," I said. "She was doing well, but there's evidence that she was running out of steam."

We discussed Gerry's legacy. Often we leave no trace of our personal history beyond our children and the stories of our life that they might tell. But Gerry's story tugged at the heartstrings of a wide community of family, friends, and hikers. Her legacy should be to pass on the lessons learned from her ordeal. She last attempted to text her husband on August 6, 2013. Her last consecutive journal entry was dated August 10, with one more entry on August 18. If her dates were correct, Gerry survived nearly three weeks in the wilderness alone.

Exactly three years after Gerry wrote the note in her journal for a would-be discoverer, I found myself alone, standing at her tent site. After more than a year of research, and having had the opportunity to learn about her through her friends, hikers, and those who had searched for her, I hoped to paint a picture of her lonely time on that hilltop. Her tent site is hallowed ground for me, so I moved off a short distance. I spent the night there, open to the darkness, within sight of where her tent once stood, and where she carefully wrote her goodbyes in her journal.

Biographers invite their subjects into their minds, their homes, and their hearts. They get to know them, sometimes better than they do their friends. Author Susie Boyt once wrote, "For a biographer, the gradual awareness of strong loyalties to your subject can be a powerful thing."

Late in that evening, I sat upon a log and leaned against an ancient birch tree. I could smell the musty fungus that grows under the peeling birch bark, and it smelled good. Just off to the north, a barred owl called, and I remembered my father telling me the owls were calling, "Who cooks for you? Who cooks for you?" I wondered if the same owl had been there while Gerry was; it's possible, if the density and diversity of prey was sustained.

My eyes adjusted to the waning light. With my journal spanning my knees, I could feel the sadness. I'm not a religious fellow, but in that moment I sensed Gerry's faith. Worse, I felt her resignation. It was perplexing. As darkness descended, I felt a burden, like a weight. I felt a sense of profound sadness that I hadn't known since my parents had passed away. I thought that was odd since I had never met Gerry.

I felt strongly at the time that her final hours had passed at night, but I don't know why. Perhaps because when I had been there alone it was getting dark. I wrote what I felt. The following is from my journal, dated August 8, 2016, 8:30 p.m.:

Gerry was effervescent. According to her friends, life had been a vivid thing to her. It is our choice to appreciate every precious moment in life, though few do so. By all accounts, Gerry seemed to cherish her family, friends, and her time on Earth. She saw the world for all its gifts—the birds, the plants, the scenery . . . even the pebbles on the ground—and followed her dream. Her journal entry three years ago was so elegant—so brave—that it seems all hardship was embraced and she surrendered to the inevitable.

I believe some time after August 6th, 2013, zipped up in her sleeping bag, prayers were offered, calling for courage. Her breathing would have become shallow and labored. Gerry found her escape from the days of helplessness, and everything and everyone she thought about made her darkened world more bright, like passing, shining moments. In the misty fog of a half-conscious state, without her knowing, her heart simply stopped.

In the end, hidden in the darkest of places, one hopes Gerry found faith and grace to be her greatest comfort. All pain passes in the end. I imagine with her eyes closed and a sense of all being well, she saw light and her fear of darkness fell away forever. I hope it did.

Love is a treasure, often given in silence, and its offer is not constrained by time or distance . . . or death. Alone in the forest, knowing the end was near, I also hope that she could somehow feel her family's love and that the family has come to terms with the loss that was truly theirs.

If a single person reads Gerry's story, and if it helps them should they become lost in the woods, I believe I know what she'd say: *That's brilliant!*

A dream can be a rare gift; we believe in it, hold on to it, and pursue it—sometimes for decades—and in the slightest moment, it can be gone. Sometime in August 2013, Gerry died in her sleeping bag. The world was hers no longer. But perhaps she can carry on. She spent a lifetime caring for and engaging people from all walks of life. Through her story, she has already changed the lives of several of the hikers she met along the trail. They hike safer. They take a little more time to look at the flowers. They smile when they see an inchworm. God knows she changed the lives of her friends, just by knowing her.

For the hikers she met, the joy of knowing Gerry along the trail was not halved by her death but doubled by the inspiration she gave them and by her lessons offered still.

In 2016, George Largay was interviewed for a YMCA video. When speaking of the loss of Gerry, his wife and his best friend for forty-five years, he said something I'll always remember. He spoke of what life was going to be like without his wife: "Faith, family, fitness, and friends. It never gets easy, but it gets *easier*. An experience like that can either make you bitter or it can make you better. And I'm focusing on the better."

Epilogue

Tell me, and I forget. Teach me, and I remember. Involve me, and I learn.

—Benjamin Franklin

In the fall of 2017, the day before Halloween, an unusual meteorological event sometimes referred to as a "bomb cyclone" hit the state of Maine. The nickname stems from a phenomenon called "bombogenesis," in which atmospheric pressure drops relatively quickly (technically, twenty-four millibars in twenty-four hours), whipping up sudden, strong winds that rocked the entire state.

Tropical Storm Philippe played a key role in the windstorm's development, as it merged with a cold front that had been moving eastward from the Midwest over the previous days. As Philippe, a relatively weak cyclone, moved northeast over south Florida toward the mid-Atlantic, its tropical moisture fed the intensity of the advancing cold front, causing the rapid drop in air pressure and resulting powerful winds that made their way north. When it hit Maine, the hurricane gusts of more than seventy-three miles per hour felled trees, downed power lines across the state, and caused flash floods. Trains couldn't run for three days. In harbors along the coast, the coast guard reported more than fifty vessels torn from their moorings.

Nine days after the storm, Doug Comstock, Dennis Haug, and I hiked back to Gerry's site with Maine television host and producer Bill Green and his cinematographer and producer, Kirk Cratty. Since 2000, Bill has produced *Bill Green's Maine*, and he has two Regional Emmys and an Edward R. Murrow Award under his belt. He is something of an institution in Maine.

We parked in the same place we had when accompanying Dottie and Mark Rust to the site and again on our first trip in with Dennis.

"This is too far in the woods," Bill commented as we donned our blaze orange clothing required in Maine during hunting season. "We won't see any hunters. No one would want to deal with dragging out a deer from this far in the woods." He was correct.

It was a beautiful day. The woods smelled sweet as they do every fall, and the wind had blown all the leaves off the maples, making them appear cold. The cool, crisp air felt clean. It was a nice day for a hike.

As we walked up Railroad Road, then northbound on the Appalachian Trail and into Gerry's campsite, the devastation of the wind storm was apparent. The trail itself was in good shape, but as we forded the two brooks and climbed the ridge to the wooden memorial where Gerry's tent had stood, the woods looked different. I had gotten used to this place by now, especially after spending my night there alone, when I had dallied both coming and going, exploring the area on my own.

We stood right on top of the site but didn't recognize it; trees were knocked down all along the top of the ridge. The wind had come from the southeast, laying the trees neatly pointing northwest, as if loggers had laid them in position for the horses to twitch them out of the forest. Doug and Dennis saw the tent site first. The white two-by-four cross placed there by Gerry's family had been crushed by a small pine, the only tree not laying in the same direction as the others. Bill wondered whether perhaps it would be fitting to let nature—the nature she loved—reclaim the site.

"No." I said. "I read in an interview that Gerry's daughter, Kerry, and her husband, Ryan, hope to someday bring their children to the site, to show them how brave their grandmother was in her most trying time. I want them to have the best chance of finding the exact spot."

Dennis, one of the navy employees who had been so emotionally invested in the search for Gerry, had already set to work trying to cut the pine with a camping tool. For the next half hour, we policed the area, removed the fallen pine tree, and repaired the wooden cross as best we could.

I suppose Gerry's beautifully written journal ought to be left private, for her family and descendants only, and while I understand why the family would want most of her final words to remain personal messages to them alone, I believe her words could have a positive effect on others. Words that regard what she felt as the days ticked by and how she arrived at her decisions.

From the information we have, perhaps we can glean enough from her ordeal to remember what to do upon becoming lost:

- Use whatever means possible to *stay calm*. Before heading out on the hike, practice how you might calm yourself if you were to find yourself disoriented.

- *Stay put* the moment you realize you're lost, provided you have water for a day or two. *Don't wander too far*. Staying put only works if somebody knows your starting point and destination. If no one knows where you are and when you are due out (someone should be informed), then find water and follow it downstream (or down a drainage in drier climates), but be careful of your feet (skirt the swamps), or you could lose a shoe.

- If you don't have a tent, build a *shelter*.

- Make a fire, contain it, and be prepared to *keep it going*.

- If you feel compelled to rely on technology, then it would be wise to invest in a personal locator beacon—such as the SPOT Satellite GPS Messenger—learn to set it up, and carry it with you.

Of course, Gerry's greatest lesson is for us to learn to navigate with a compass and be aware of our location, wherever we may be. Appalachian Trail Conservancy executive and author Brian King oversees publication of the ATC's series of official maps, considered essential hiking materials for both thru- and section hikers. Each state's map overlaps with neighboring maps. All along the trail surrounding areas and additional side trails are also included, along with contours and elevations. The official maps weigh only an average of 24.4 grams each. Yet many hikers don't carry them, for a variety of reasons.

Found among Gerry's belongings at her tent site was one of the ATC official maps for Maine. It was so sodden, so rotten, that it was difficult to make out whether it was the correct map for the section where she became lost (no. 6). Even if it was, a hiker must know *where* they are on the map. To aid in their self-rescue, they must be spatially oriented to begin with. North of the trail? South? Gerry knew she was "north of woods road"—Railroad Road. Sadly, by the time she may have decided to try to follow the brook to safety—if she considered that at all—weakness had descended upon her. So much in life is timing.

In his first two years of retirement from the navy and the SERE school, Dennis let his disappointment from the search inspire him. He wanted something positive to come out of it. He enrolled in a master's program, and he made a plan.

After our hike in to Gerry's site with Bill Green, Dennis told me of his plan: "It's a contribution, really," he said. "It's a way I might be able to help some people. I'm going to start a school of my own, with different options—orienteering, wilderness survival . . . self-rescue."

"That's a great idea," I told him.

"I'll run it like a business so that it's feasible for me to do it for a long time." Dennis looked up Railroad Road, toward Mount Redington. "Maybe I can help someone."

I hoped he would follow through with his plan. A year later, he sent me an e-mail:

Dennis' School of Survival and Consulting or better known as DSSC is an innovative organization that puts its students in various true-to-life survival situations demanding sound leadership, teamwork, critical thinking, improvisation and problem solving through unique challenges designed to test the vary basis of survival. We offer basic classroom courses with instructor demonstration, field-based station training with student demonstration, scenario-based tailored training to the more advanced customer, and high-intensity team building training. In addition to survival programs, we build upon basic Wilderness Medicine certifications teaching remote and improvised medicine courses utilizing the self-

aid and buddy-aid philosophies. The school was inspired by a search for a missing Appalachian Trail hiker that lasted more than 3 years resulting in the recovery of her remains. The mission is to prepare people for safe and enjoyable outdoor experiences regardless of the environment or conditions. The emphasis is on basic survival principles geared towards AT, PCT, CDT hikers, as well as campers, adventurers, and survivalist alike.

I was happy to read it. He had even written a business model. When he's up and running, I plan on sending my twenty-three-year-old son and nineteen-year-old daughter. I'm sure they'll like to go.

On one of my first research trips to the area, Doug Comstock and I hiked into Poplar Ridge Lean-To near the end of May 2016. The north side of Poplar was still covered in two to three feet of wet, hard-packed snow. It was raining, about forty degrees, and quite miserable. In a downpour, Doug got a roaring fire going in the hearth in front of the lean-to. Once we had eaten supper, Doug pulled from his pack a small, framed photo of Gerry. It was a printout of Dottie Rust's photograph. Holes had been predrilled into the frame. Doug found an out-of-the-way spot on the wall of the lean-to (on the side where Gerry had slept) and screwed the photo to the wall. I e-mailed the Maine Appalachian Trail Club and told them about it and offered that, if they'd rather it not be there, they would need a number 2 Phillips head screwdriver to remove it. I received no reply. As of spring 2018, it was still there.

The next day, after wading across a very swollen Orbeton Stream, Doug and I hiked back toward the car. As we left the spot where the AT crosses Railroad Road, the sun came out, warming our faces but doing nothing for our soaked clothes. A little bird flew to a branch next to the trail, only a few feet from our faces. I had never seen that species of bird before. It must have been curious; it flitted around but stayed very close to us. We were both surprised at how unafraid it seemed.

Then, as we walked, it went along with us.

We hiked fast to try to warm up. The little songbird flew from branch to branch, keeping up with us—not ahead of us, not behind us—and too close to us to seem natural.

After a quarter mile of its company, I said, "Did I mention, Gerry loved birds?"

Doug stopped, and the bird stopped with him. He held out his hand, but the bird didn't come. It regarded Doug, looking him up and down, and flew away.

"Interesting," he said.

Acknowledgments

For their advice and perspective and for their patience with my asking a multitude of questions, I am deeply grateful to Tim McElhannon, Dottie and Mark Rust, Regina Clark, Terry Bliss, Kit Parks, Mary Blanton, Katharine Armijo, Mike Jurasius, Bobby Thompson and Lee Thompson, and Dianne Cook.

Many thanks to my agent, Paul Lucas, at Janklow & Nesbit for his confidence and patience and to Michael Steere at Down East Books for his faith in this book.

This book would not be worth reading if not for the help of first readers John Holyoke, Monica Coffee, Alan Comeau, and Tim McElhannon, who saved me from redundancies and typographical imbecilities.

I am grateful to Betty Anne Schenk and to Jane Lee, who unselfishly shared so much of their love for Gerry. I am afraid some of this book will be difficult for them, but both agreed early on that if Gerry could help one soul in the future through her ordeal, she would not hesitate to do so. Thank you to Doug Comstock for his help with research, his companionship, and his stories. He kept me awake on the long drives, expounded on the virtues of microbreweries, and showed an unwavering compassion for Gerry's struggles.

Special gratitude is owed to Lieutenant Kevin Adam of the Maine Warden Service for talking about a difficult subject, of which he was likely already tired; to Lieutenant Commander J. D. Walker, Dennis Haug, and Brett Pehowic, and to Maine Warden Debbie Palman (Ret.) and all the wardens and volunteers who participated in the search for Gerry; also to Warden Dave Georgia (Ret.) for much support and to Cathie Pelletier for her guidance.

Thank you to Father Frank Murray and Father Tim Nadeau for helping me investigate the mysteries of dying within the faith of the Church of Rome. Also, thanks go to Jon Piper, Esq., who knows why—or should—and to Abderrahmane Dakir for his poetry.

I am grateful to Bob Elfstrom, Brian King, and Warren Doyle for their sage advice and to Doctors John Frankland, Lloyd Harmon, S. Craige Williamson, Paul Denoncourt, Peter Copithorne, and Bruce Hamilton-Dick for their continued help and support.

I sourced and benefited from published work by the *New York Times*, the *Washington Post*, the *Tennessean*, Radcliffe Institute, Harvard University, Harvard Medical School, Fox News, William Syrotuck, Dr. Ken Hill, Saint Mary's University (Halifax), the Mountain Rescue England and Wales, Northumberland National Park SRT, Centre for Search Research (United Kingdom), the International Search and Rescue Advisory Group, US National Association of Search and Rescue, Royal Canadian Mounted Police, David B. Field, Debbie Palman, David Miller, Susie Boyt, Donn Fendler and Joseph Egan, the *Boston Globe*, the *Portland Press Herald*, the *Bangor Daily News*, the *Lewiston Sun Journal*, Owen Beattie and John Geiger's *Frozen in Time: The Fate of the Franklin Expedition*, *The Bollard*, the *Kennebec Journal*, the Appalachian Trail Conservancy Archives, the Library of Congress, *The Trek* blog, Zach Davis, Bob Bowie, Verizon Digital Media Services, the Brentwood Home Page, Pierre Berton, the US Navy, Alfred Binet's work in *La Revue Psychologique*, the *New York Daily News*, WhiteBlaze.net, AnimalPlanet.com, the US Department of Homeland Security, Bowdoin College Collections, the Maine State Library, *National Geographic*, and the Oregon Health and Science University Library.

A word of thanks is owed to Dave Dumas, Dan Feldman, Tom Bieber, Roger Kruppa, Steven Magee, Steve Mittman, Christopher Desmond, Oscar Emerson, Alicia Byrne, Rudy Maxa, Gary Drinkwater, Lyn Asselta, Bonnie Galayda (for her attic room to write in), and the entire staff of the operating room at the Everett Hospital campus of the Cambridge Health Alliance.

And a special thanks to Lisa, Sam, and Hazen, for allowing me to work seven days a week for two years.

About the Author

Denis "Dee" Dauphinee has been a mountaineering, fly-fishing, and back-country guide and a photographer for more than thirty years, and he has participated in several search-and-rescue organizations. He has led many expeditions, including mountain, jungle, or desert treks, on four continents. He has four first-ascents on mountains and has climbed above 20,000 feet thirteen times. He has published scores of magazine and newspaper articles, as well as *Stoneflies & Turtleheads* (a collection of fly-fishing and travel essays), *The River Home* (a novel), and *Highlanders Without Kilts* (an award-winning work of historical fiction about a Canadian family's ordeal and a Nova Scotia battalion's odyssey during World War I). He lives in middle Maine.

For further reading about the history of the Appalachian Trail, please visit Dee's website: www.ddauphinee.com.